Silverstone's
First Grand Prix
1948
The Race on the Runways

**Anthony Meredith &
Gordon Blackwell**

AMBERLEY

For Sir Stirling Moss, who led the first laps

ever raced at Silverstone

Front and back cover: Both paintings of the start of
the race are by kind permission of the artist, Michael
Turner. The originals hang in the Segrave Room of the
Royal Automobile Club, Pall Mall, and the British Racing
Drivers' Clubhouse at Silverstone.

First published 2014

Amberley Publishing
The Hill, Stroud
Gloucestershire, GL5 4EP

www.amberley-books.com

Copyright © Anthony Meredith & Gordon Blackwell, 2014

The right of Anthony Meredith & Gordon Blackwell to be identified as the Authors
of this work has been asserted in accordance with the Copyrights, Designs and
Patents Act 1988.

ISBN 978 1 4456 1776 3 (print)
ISBN 978 1 4456 1794 7 (ebook)

British Library Cataloguing in Publication Data.
A catalogue record for this book is available from the British Library.

Typesetting by Amberley Publishing.
Printed in the UK.

ACKNOWLEDGEMENTS

Anthony Meredith wrote the text. Gordon Blackwell was an invaluable helper in its research.

Special thanks go to Joe Pettican and Sian Griffiths at Amberley Publishing. David Ellsmore-Petty and John Pearson both made contributions of real significance to the project. Michael Turner most kindly allowed the use of three of his superb paintings. Stephanie Sykes has been very supportive at the British Racing Drivers' Club (BRDC) Archives. Sir Stirling Moss could not have been more helpful or generous with his time. Reminiscences from Gordon Watson's widow, Marjorie, and George Nixon's daughter, Ruth, were also highlights along the way.

Photographs were kindly supplied by Ian Brown, the BRDC Archives, Graham Churchill, D. Hyslop, Getty Images, Michael Hammond (The Guy Griffiths Collection), Chris Kelley/Fantasy Club, the Ludvigsen Library at the Revs Institute for Automotive Research, Ruth Mockett, John Pearson, the Royal Automobile Club (RAC), Ted Walker (Ferret Fotographics), Marjorie Watson and Kent Robinson. We have endeavoured to find out and advertise all illustrative sources, but would be grateful to be told of any instances in which we have failed to properly acknowledge other people's work, despite our best intentions and efforts. Any such omissions will be rectified in any subsequent editions.

We are most grateful for help from Heather, Jo and Michael Meredith; Jonathan, Doreen and Geoff Blackwell; the BRDC; the Library of Churchill College, Cambridge; the British Library; T. C. Harrison Ltd; Haymarket Publishing; the RAC; Sergio Angelini; Simonetta Berbeglia; Sophie Bridges; Ivy Cakebread Stephanie Chamberlain; Graham and Brenda Churchill; Cesare de Agostini; Trevor Dunmore; Sandy Fage; Heidi Hennessy; Jaap Horst; Genevieve Mahoney; Lucy McCarthy; Tim Metcalfe; Ruth Mockett; Jayme Moore; Paul Nixon; Martina Oliver; Tim Parnell; Stuart Pringle; Garry Rankin; Kent Robinson; Bruce K. Trenery; Marjorie Watson; Sarah Weech; Kevin Wood; David Wesley; Rex Woodgate and Liz Zettl.

Among many helpful books were Cesare de Agostini's *Villoresi: Il 'Gigi' Nazionale* and *Ascari: Un Mito Italiano*, Sheldon & Rabagliati's *The Record of Grand Prix Racing*, Anthony Pritchard's *Racers*, Graham Gauld's *Reg Parnell*, the BRDC's *Silverstone: 50 Golden Years*, Karl Ludvigsen's *Alberto Ascari*, Kevin Desmond's *The Man With Two Shadows*, Peter Carrick's *Silverstone*, Princess Ceril's *The Prince and I*, Raymond Mays' *Split Seconds*, Piers Brendon's *The Motoring Century*, Giovanni Lurani's *La Storia della Mille Miglia*, John Bolster's *Motoring is My Business*, J. A. Salkeld's *The Start of Something Big* and Guy Griffiths' *1946 and All That*. Back issues of *Motor Sport*, *The Motor*, *The Autocar*, *Tatler*, the *Buckingham Advertiser*, *The Northampton Chronicle & Echo* and *The Times* were also most helpful.

CHAPTER 1

Francis Curzon, the 5th Earl Howe, was standing on a kitchen chair by the side of the perimeter road of an old airfield. In front of him were twenty-five racing cars, spaced five and four abreast in alternate lines. It was nearly 2.00 p.m. on Saturday 2 October 1948. The first Grand Prix ever to be held at Silverstone would start as soon as the sixty-four-year-old Earl gave the signal.

With a minute to go, twenty-four engines, audible several miles away, screamed into life together. Only one machine remained silent: an old Maserati, on the far side of the track near the back, which was pushed onto the narrow strip of grass in front of a crowd standing seven or eight deep. The young and inexperienced Roy Salvadori had oiled a sparking plug and would need a push to the nearby pits. Howe could sense his frustration, even at a distance.

In pole position, just a few yards away from Howe, was Frenchman Louis Chiron in his Lago-Talbot. Always carefully dressed, Chiron wore a linen head-covering of a delicate pale blue that perfectly matched his beautiful Lago-Talbot. Now a forty-nine year old, but still as keen as ever to be the centre of attention, Chiron was conveying in vigorous mime his last-minute anxieties to two mechanics, who were yet to sully their white silk overalls. His team's patron, Paul Vallée, a burly

figure in a brightly-checked jacket and white panama, hovered nearby with the air of an anxious on-course bookie.

Chiron's Talbot would be the first of several machines to rush past the wooden chair, but there was no trace of anxiety on Howe's face. Behind the round, tortoise-shell spectacles, indeed, his eyes were justly sparkling, for this was an event that could not possibly have taken place without him. It was Howe, for example, who had encouraged Louis Chiron to forsake for one weekend the glamorous street circuits he so loved for a forlorn former aerodrome that RAF Bomber Command had created in an obscure part of the South Midlands. And there were six other drivers from Europe. Next to Chiron on the front row was a thirty-four-year-old Swiss Baron, Emmanuel 'Toulo' de

Opposite left: The map of the circuit from a heavily thumbed race programme.

Opposite right: Francis Curzon, the 5th Earl Howe, captured in characteristic good humour (eight years after the race) by Ralph Sallon. (*Motor-Racing Past and Present, BP/Shellmex, 1956*)

ENCLOSURE C

COPSE CORNER

ENCLOSURE B

WOODCOTE

ENCLOSURE D

SEGRAVE STRAIGHT

MAGGOTS CORNER

GRAND STAND COVERED

PITS AREA

LUFFIELD ABBEY FARM

CONTROL TOWER

ENCLOSURE F

GRAND STAND UNCOVERED

START

SEGRAVE CORNER

BECKETTS CORNER

ABBEY CURVE

CHAPEL CURVE

ENCLOSURE A

SEAMAN CORNER

ENCLOSURE E

SEAMAN STRAIGHT

HANGAR STRAIGHT

N
W   E
S

RAC

CLUB CORNER

STOWE CORNER

SILVERSTONE

SCALE IN FEET
0 100 200 300 400 500 600 700 800 900 1000

Graffenried, in his much-raced Maserati; and alongside, another French veteran in another new Lago-Talbot, Philippe Étancelin, who, at fifty-one, still spent the summers racing and the winters running his Normandy estate and managing his business in the wool trade.

Further back on the grid, on the third row, were two forty-two-year-olds, Gianfranco Comotti and Louis Rosier. 'Franco' Comotti had made a name for himself in the 1930s in Enzo Ferrari's Alfa Romeos before quitting Mussolini's Italy and settling in France, where Talbot's owner, Antonio Lago, employed him as a test driver. He returned to his homeland during the war, however, as a secret agent, passing on to the Allies information gained from his position in the Italian navy. He had subsequently operated in North Italy, reporting on the Nazis' movements there, until captured by the Gestapo in February 1944. Sentenced to death, he was given a mysterious reprieve, perhaps through the help of his racing driver wife, known as 'La Marocchina' (the Lady from Morocco) because of her dark good looks. After the war, he returned to Paris and, working for Talbot, was in the right place to get a drive (sponsored by a mysterious Italian businessman) in Lago's new Grand Prix contender, the 26C. The small and dark Comotti still looked more like a spy in the movies than a racing driver, with his hollow cheeks, sleek, receding hair and an understandably haunted look. He was seldom without a cigarette.

Another inveterate smoker, Louis Rosier, had built up a prosperous garage in Clermont Ferrand in the 1930s, the base for his racing activities. He had fought in the French army before the Nazi conquest, after which he helped the Resistance all he could. Eventually, in the autumn of 1943, betrayed by an informer, he found himself at the front of his garage face to face with the Gestapo.

'Where is the proprietor?' they asked him.

'I'll go and find him, messieurs,' replied Rosier, hastily rushing out of the back of the garage. Getting a lift from a passing van, he escaped to the hills, but his wife was arrested and imprisoned in Germany. The devastated Rosier became a Resistance leader, risking his life again and again with the Maquis. On France's liberation, he set out for Germany in search of his wife. Reaching Buchenwald just days after it had been liberated, he learnt that she had been taken from there to a camp in Czechoslovakia. Miraculously, he found her.

Howe's eye lingered approvingly on Comotti and Rosier. How fitting that these two men who had fought so bravely against fascism should now be at the heart of an English grid with their French Talbots surrounded by English cars and drivers! There, on the row in front of them, was Maj. Tony Rolt, still a serving Army officer, six times an escapee from German POW camps before being sent to Colditz; and on the row behind was Bob Ansell, who, in the famous retreat from Dunkirk, had resourcefully saved a whole platoon by commandeering two tiny fishing boats.

Howe's greatest acquisition, however, had been two of the very latest Maseratis to be driven by Luigi Villoresi and Alberto Ascari. He knew Villoresi well. They had often raced together on the continent in the 1930s, and Gigi (as Luigi was always known) had raced in England before, twice at Crystal Palace. He had also climbed Shelsey's famous hill. The war, of course, had been a terrible setback for him. Howe knew little of the details of Villoresi and Ascari's joint wartime venture, except that it involved helping the Italian army in North Africa. Gigi was tight-lipped about both this and the time he spent as a POW when his hair had turned to silver.

Howe was intrigued by Alberto Ascari. His famous father, Antonio Ascari, had been one of the great Italian drivers of the 1920s before his tragic death. He knew, too, that Gigi, Alberto's mentor, believed that one day the son would eclipse the father, and, from what he'd seen of the young Ascari, he could understand Gigi's enthusiasm.

The sun was now out, but a breeze was making its presence felt across Silverstone's flat expanses, fully justifying Howe's woolly cardigan. Short and stocky, with his favourite flat cap at its usual jaunty angle and a crumpled race programme sticking out of one of the pockets of his sports jacket, Howe looked every inch the relaxed country gentleman that he had indeed become in 1929 on inheriting his father's title. It had been a life-changing moment. Up till then, as Viscount Curzon, educated at Eton and Oxford, he had followed the kind of career appropriate to Winston Churchill's first cousin and a descendant of a British naval hero at the time of Lord Nelson, serving first as a regular officer in the Royal Navy and fighting with distinction in the First World War, and afterwards as an MP. But the death of his father had suddenly given him the means to change course and devote himself to motor racing, the all-consuming passion he had hitherto largely suppressed. The Buckinghamshire estate that he had inherited might end up a little the worse for his desire to further British prestige on the racetracks of Europe, but that single-minded desire was irresistible.

Though only starting seriously when in his forties, he was soon making an impact at home and abroad, winning Le Mans

Earl Howe, as depicted in the 1934 cigarette card series 'Champions'.

in 1931. He loved road racing on the continent, and tried hard to reverse the ban in Britain. In 1932, he championed a compromise, a road circuit in Richmond Park 'from Robin Hood Gate, straight across the park, down to Kingston and back again'. Although he was foiled in this, by the age of fifty he had himself become 'one of the greatest drivers of the world', at least according to a cigarette card of 1934: 'Earl Howe must be considered unfortunate, for he has had more than his fair share of accidents inseparable from high-speed motoring. He is quite fearless, and the fact that he has escaped death by inches and seconds on many occasions does nothing to deter him.'

It was almost time to start the race. How many of the machines facing him were old friends! Particularly the ERAs, those wonderful creations of Raymond Mays and the factory he had built in the orchard of his Lincolnshire home! There, on the third row, ready to sweep past his chair, was the very ERA he himself had bought from Raymond and raced with the works team. He'd had it painted in his own colours of blue and black, of course, but now for the current owner, Cuth Harrison, it was dark green. What a joy to see the old car here, even if Cuth had given it some modernistic front bodywork!

How many of the drivers, too, he had known as fellow competitors! There, on the inside of the second row with a new Maserati, was a good friend, the Siamese Prince Bira – it had been when fighting Bira for the lead at Brooklands that he had had one of his most painful accidents. And there, surprisingly far back, was Raymond Mays, in his black and silver ERA. How many years had he had that great car? How many years was it since his break-up with Humphrey Cook and the ERA company? What a talent Ray had for getting sponsorship! What

a triumph to have run ERA so long on Cook's money! And how he admired the burning patriotism that fired all Mays' financial deals! Still racing at forty-nine and the current British hill-climb champion, yet, at the same time, fully engrossed in his latest patriotic venture, the founding of BRM! But it looked possible from the sudden commotion around Ray that he might just have stalled? Mechanics were rushing up to him. Poor Ray! At least all was well at the front. Chiron's mechanics and Paul Vallée had finally fled from the grid. It was precisely two o'clock. Time to raise the Union Jack and hold it high.

The much-anticipated moment had finally arrived: a post-war Grand Prix on British soil! Might Silverstone one day fill the role of Brooklands as the home of British motor racing? It had to be possible. But a roar of racing engines, rising in anguish to an ear-splitting crescendo, drew Howe back to the business in hand and, with the finest of flourishes, he dropped his Union Jack.

CHAPTER 2

Three months earlier, on 30 June, there was little traffic on London's streets as members of the motoring press approached the Royal Automobile Club in Pall Mall. Petrol, like so much else, was strictly rationed, available only by coupon. However, though the city might have been strangely still, as if brooding on its many untouched bomb sites, the journalists entering the club looked distinctly cheerful. They were there (so they thought) to be introduced to the Royal Automobile Club's new Competitions Manager, Col. Stanley Barnes, and cocktails were promised. The RAC's Edwardian opulence always made a refreshing oasis in the current desert of austerity, the spirit of a more glorious past prevailing amid all the fine paintings, cases of silver trophies and, not least, the Art Deco statue of Britannia, 'The Guardian of the Seas', that Lord Howe had given in memory of his father. Some carpets might have seemed a little worn, and some paintwork less than fresh. Tapioca pudding and bubble and squeak might somehow have invaded the luncheon menu. And yet, all things considered, the RAC still stood bravely for the old values.

The journalists were ushered into the elegant Mall Room, where the club's chairman, Wilfrid Andrews, smart in a dark double-breasted suit, welcomed them in his usual forthright manner – hands behind his back, not a note in sight. A burly man of fifty-six who liked his cigars and brandy, Andrews had been chairman for three years and intended to remain so for many more. He had no particular love of motor sport – for recreation he preferred golf and Tom Whittaker's Arsenal – but he had a shrewd feeling for the club's best interests. He talked eloquently as he introduced his new appointee, Col. Barnes, standing dutifully at his side with bald head gleaming in the light of a chandelier. The journalists, for their part, were distinctly curious. They knew Stan Barnes well. He'd been a racing driver and team manager in the pre-war days. Undoubtedly a good type. But why all the fuss?

It was soon apparent. In the past, began Andrews, the RAC, as British motor sport's controlling body, had been content to leave the operation of the racing circuits to private enterprise. However, with the loss of all the pre-war venues, the club had felt it could no longer tolerate the damage being done to British prestige abroad. Then came the big announcement: 'We have entered into negotiations with the Air Ministry for the lease of Silverstone Airfield in the Midlands. Negotiations are already 99 per cent complete. The financial obligations will be shouldered by the Club.' Andrews paused to enjoy the reaction before paying a quick compliment to Earl Howe's involvement, alluding mysteriously that he could not be present, being 'abroad on business not unconnected with Silverstone'. Then came the second big announcement: 'It is our intention to stage a British Grand Prix event within the course of a month or two.' The excited response that this received could surely have been heard by 'The Guardian of the Seas' down in the basement.

Stanley Barnes took over, standing by a large map. Silverstone, he explained, would simulate a road circuit in its use of both the aerodrome's perimeter road and two of the three runways. The longest runway measured 2,000 yards and was conveniently intersected by the other two. Any number of interesting circuit configurations were possible, but the one chosen – as indicated on the map – would result in a lap of over 3½ miles. As regards the names of corners, several would commemorate local features such as Seven Copses Wood, Maggot's Moor and the former Chapel of Thomas à Becket. Then there were the last two British winners of a Grand Prix, Henry Segrave and Dick Seaman, commemorated by the two hairpin bends at the centre of the circuit. There was also a little self-promotion: the first corner would be named after Woodcote Park, the RAC's country club near Epsom, and Club Corner would reflect the nearby enclosure reserved for Full and Associate RAC members.

As the news spread, Wilfrid Andrews naturally gained rather more of the credit than Howe. Andrews was already the dominant figure in the club. Previous RAC chairmen had to pay careful heed to their secretaries, but Andrews had shrewdly promoted the gentle Geoffrey Samuelson, a secretary who would never say boo to the chairman's goose, so Andrews' self-promotional schemes flourished. 'There is no limit to what you can do,' he once admitted with a smile, 'if you take credit for other people's ideas!' The resourceful Howe kept feeding the chairman with them.

Howe himself also made well-judged public interventions. Only that January, in opening an exhibition at Earl's Court organised by the British Racing Drivers' Club (of which he was founder-president), he had highlighted the disaster of Brooklands' closure. Stirred up by this, *The Times* wrote a powerful leader:

Motor racing has never been regarded with favour on the mainland of the British Isles where it has been confined to a few private tracks and road circuits – none of them now available – and short inadequate hill-climbs and special trial courses. On the Continent and in Ulster, Jersey and the Isle of Man official permission is given to close public roads in order to hold motor races, with the result that the sport has gained a popularity abroad which is not always appreciated in this country. The big Grand Prix races of France, Belgium, Switzerland and Italy are national events that attract enormous crowds and although the competing cars are entered by firms, syndicates and private individuals, and not by national organisations, it is inevitable that they should be closely associated, in the minds of the spectators, with the countries of origin…

Since the war British racing drivers, forced to use cars designed and built before 1939, have been outclassed in all the important races except when they have been driving foreign cars. The sight of the British finishing at the tail of the fields, while rousing the sympathy and admiration of knowledgeable spectators for the gallantry of the drivers in face of hopeless odds, has at the same time appeared a reflection of Britain's position as a great industrial power…

Six months of hard canvassing had followed. In March 1948, *Motor Sport*'s young editor, Bill Boddy, wrote an inflammatory piece expressing his shock that racing was again flourishing in Germany: 'While Britain has no place where the BRM can be tested, these German enthusiasts go racing even in the British zone' and 'German racing drivers apparently find the public so keen on motor-racing that they are doing very nicely'. 'Curious,' he ended bitterly, 'for, after all, Britain did win the war.'

That April, too, Howe and Reg Parnell had led a campaign on behalf of Donington Park, supported by influential drivers like Raymond Mays, Prince Bira and Bob Gerard. When, 'despite the eloquent pleading of Mays,' the parish council had decided to make Donington a permanent vehicle depot, Howe knew the time had come to play his trump card: the RAC and Wilfrid Andrews.

Shortly after the press party at Pall Mall, the RAC confirmed that a twelve-month trial rental of Silverstone had been agreed with the Air Ministry. The rent alone would cost £600. The suggestion of a Grand Prix in a month's time had been a little over-optimistic, but a date was now fixed, only three months away. *The Motor* was 'staggered'. *Motor Sport* found it all 'breathtaking'.

Howe's 'business not unconnected with Silverstone' had taken him in his pre-war V12 Lagonda to the San Remo Grand Prix on the Italian Riviera. Though the sport's international controlling body, the FIA, would wait till 1950 before starting a World Championship, San Remo was part of a vigorous third season of post-war Grand Prix racing in Europe and attracted huge crowds. There were three days to go before to the Pall Mall announcement to the press, so Howe had to bide his time and speak obliquely. Meanwhile, he noted with approval the brand-new Maseratis that Ascari and Villoresi brought home in 1st and 2nd places.

The next week he was in Switzerland for the European Grand Prix at Bremgarten (outside Berne), where he was able to make

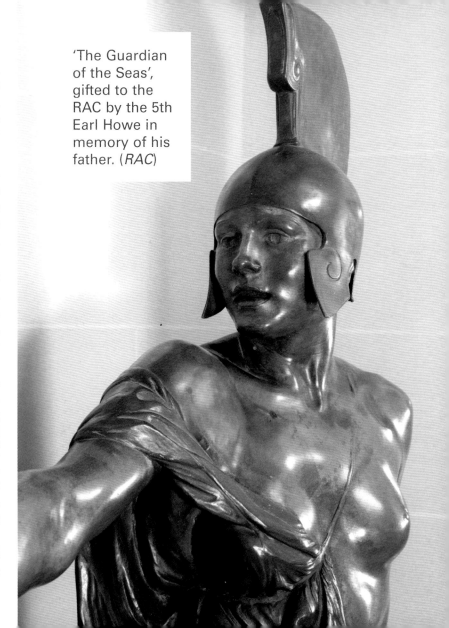

'The Guardian of the Seas', gifted to the RAC by the 5th Earl Howe in memory of his father. (*RAC*)

his big pitch. Howe now let it be known that the starting money would be a generous £200 for all foreign drivers, a figure that matched most of the continental circuits; all expenses would be paid. There would be equally excellent prize money (£500 for the winner and graded amounts for the next nine places) as well as £25 for fastest lap of the race.

Howe's attempts to interest Alfa Romeo were made all the more difficult by the tragic death of their top driver, Achille Varzi, in a practice crash. Howe had also been hoping to attract two wealthy Swiss drivers, Baron 'Toulo' de Graffenried and Christian Kautz, whose Maseratis were both entered by Enrico Platé, but Kautz also lost his life that weekend.

There was immediate interest from several drivers of Lago-Talbots, though Louis Chiron was unapproachable, shocked by the death of Varzi, which he himself had witnessed. Howe knew that the British public would warm to Chiron, affectionately known as *le vieux renard* for his legendary craftiness. The 'old fox' had other little eccentricities – he would sometimes stroke his cars and talk to them softly as if they were pet animals. Howe had known Chiron in the 1920s, when his Bugatti was sponsored by a rich industrialist with whose wife the handsome Frenchman was conducting an indiscreet affair. It would be good to have a big character like Chiron at Silverstone, and the ambience of Pall Mall and the RAC's country club would be just the right kind of carrot. For Chiron, who had been brought up in Monaco's Hôtel de Paris (which his father had managed), was himself a cordon bleu cook and always relished the finest things in life.

Howe made useful contact at Bremgarten with Enzo Ferrari, who, after many successful years of preparing Alfa Romeos, had finally decided to produce his own machines. The Ferrari 125 was almost ready. Two leading French drivers, Sommer and Wimille, had been approached. Farina too. Ferrari himself showed some interest in Silverstone, but it was too soon to make any commitments. The reopening of Monza, just a fortnight after the RAC's date, was his understandable priority.

The Maserati 'works' team, the Scuderia Ambrosiana of Milan, was the most enthusiastic of all. Count Giovanni 'Johnny' Lurani, a particular friend of Howe's, was the dominant figure in the Scuderia, founded in the late 1930s as a co-operative of Italian racing drivers, Villoresi among them. A great Anglophile with a perfect English accent, Lurani had persuaded Howe to lead a British attack in 1933 on Italy's greatest motor race, the Mille Miglia, he and Howe subsequently being team-mates in the K3 sports cars that MG had specially built for the race. The Lurani–Howe friendship had thereafter blossomed, Lurani writing eulogistically of his friend as *'una figura incomparabile nell' automobilismo. He was a 'grande sportivo* and a *perfetto gentiluomo'*. Howe likewise found Villoresi warmly encouraging. It would not be easy for Villoresi to get to England, for he had Formula 2 commitments in Florence the previous weekend, but he assured Howe that he would be there in one of the latest Maseratis: 'I will not let my English friends down. *Prometto.'*

Opposite left: The entrance hall of the Royal Automobile Club, with one of its striking displays.

Opposite right: The equally impressive Great Gallery. (RAC)

CHAPTER 3

Jimmy Brown, a twenty-nine-year-old no-nonsense Scotsman, walked briskly from Silverstone Village along the lane to Dadford on the first day in his new job as Track Manager. To his right were some of the buildings connected with the administration and education departments of 17 OTU, the Operations Training Unit for which the airfield had been built in 1943. Behind them, hidden away in thick woods, nearly 2,000 people had been accommodated in regulation RAF huts: the small but regular turnover of aircrews, learning how to handle Wellington bombers as a team, and those whose job it was to support them and the planes they flew from the airfield across the road.

To Brown's left, beyond a tired barbed-wire fence, was the first sign of that airfield: several large hexagonal slabs of concrete that Brown, as a former wartime pilot, recognised as a Dispersal Point, a parking area for a few of the fifty or so Wellingtons stationed at Silverstone. Weeds now were softening the harshness of the concrete, and rabbits and hares were retreating nervously to the safety of their homes, alarmed by early morning sounds. A little further on, still on his left, came the entrance to the old airfield with, just inside, the Nissen hut that had once been the all-important guardhouse. It was like entering a ghost town. So many personal hopes, ambitions, fears and tragedies now lay forgotten amid the decay. But Brown was not one to sentimentalise. He himself had survived the war and he had every intention of making a success of the peace.

He was unworried by his ignorance of motor racing. Col. Barnes, in appointing him, had given assurances that the RAC would be handling that side of things. He was simply 'the nuts-and-bolts man – the magician who waves a magic wand and ensures that all paper requests become flesh-and-blood reality!' It was an attractive challenge for a naturally incisive individual. Brown's most recent job had been in the cut-and-thrust of racehorse auctions at Tattersall's. Before flying Blenheims, Spitfires, Hurricanes and Mosquitoes in the war, he had been in the concrete business, servicing the housing industry. He was nothing if not adaptable.

He planned an early chat with those in charge of the two businesses sharing the airfield with him: the site manager of Rootes Cars, responsible for the storage in the five hangars of new Humbers awaiting export overseas; and Smith Churchill, who lived with his family in Luffield Abbey Farm as the Development Manager appointed by the Buckinghamshire Agricultural Executive. Churchill and his team had been working for the last year on the recultivation of the fields around the runways, part of a national initiative to combat food shortages.

Above: The Browns on their wedding day, 1947. (*Ian Brown*)

Right: Jimmy and Kay Brown on holiday.

Brown had ten weeks to prepare the aerodrome for the Grand Prix, after which his three-month contract (at £45 16s 8d a month) would be reviewed. He and his wife, Kay, had made arrangements to stay with friends at nearby Bleak Hall Farm. It was hardly an ideal situation for a newly married couple but the two of them were determined to meet all the challenges head-on.

To his left, as he stood looking up the entrance road, was the overgrown Dispersal Point he had spotted through the fence; to his right, the former guardhouse and, beyond it, a random complex of buildings that had once formed the aerodrome's operational heartland. Straight ahead were a few huts looking out across the perimeter road towards the flat expanse of the runways, which he recognized as the crew locker and drying rooms, where the Wellingtons' six-man crews would have assembled before being taken by buses to their planes.

He turned into the airfield's heartland, lying scattered around a straight and overgrown road that ran parallel with the Dadford lane and the future track between Woodcote and Abbey. There were well-established trees along both sides, giving the brief illusion of a rural high street or the formal avenue of a country house. And a formal avenue it had indeed once been, the old tree-lined carriage drive that Earl Temple had created in the late eighteenth century all the way between his home, Stowe House, and Silverstone village. To the immediate left was a hangar over 70 metres long. To the right, a plethora of stores and workshops; the dark steel frame of a high-level water tank tower that once held 80,000 gallons; and a brick-built parachute store of conspicuous height. To the left, a second hangar, just as long and sombre as the first, and next to it a hut once devoted to radar. This maze of derelict buildings was a worry. They might well have their uses in the longer term, but, for the immediate moment, they would only be irritating obstructions to the passage and parking of cars.

Coming to the end of the tree-lined avenue and turning round the back of the second hangar, Brown found himself at the final corner of the new track, Abbey Curve. From here, the spaciousness of the whole site was very striking; so, too, the way the ground sloped gently away to the south. To the right was the spectator area to be created for the RAC's members. What a great deal of fencing was going to have to be acquired, just for Enclosure A! But what a piece of luck that it contained another dispersal point – how useful the hard standing might be. To the left in the distance was Stowe Corner, and far away, on the horizon between Stowe and Club, a couple of Nissen huts serving as reminders that the placid fields before them had once provided underground storage for bombs.

Brown walked out on to the perimeter road at Abbey Curve. It seemed in encouragingly good condition, with no obvious signs of the asphalt revealing its concrete base. It remained in good condition, too, as he walked along the straight beyond the bend, leading to the start-line. On the right, a rising expanse of open fields; and beyond, on the brow, the cluster of sheds and buildings that was Luffield Abbey Farm with the aerodrome's four-square control tower beside it. The start-line area was Brown's biggest challenge. Stanley Barnes wanted at least one grandstand erected here, probably between the two hangars, facing the farm. He also wanted nearby pits and a footbridge crossing the track.

Opposite: The Control Tower as it was in 1949 at the time of an early VSCC meeting (*Graham Churchill*) and as it is today (*inset*).

It was clear that a team of helpers from the village would be needed to clean the whole place up. Jimmy's wife Kay was the niece of Silverstone's postmistress, so they already had some rapport with the village, and Kay's local connections were going to be crucial. Within a week of his appointment, Brown had signed on a large army of local ladies, keen to earn a few shillings at the aerodrome. Nearby building firms were likewise proving enthusiastic. Soon the RAC's Grand Prix ledger would be reflecting some of Jimmy Brown's early requirements: fifty haversacks: £7 10s 0d; fifty pickets: £4 12s 9d; one sledgehammer: 18s 6d.

* * *

Geoffrey Samuelson was another RAC employee with challenging problems. Samuelson's job as Secretary was to look after the whole of the Pall Mall operation (the club and its full members). Now, in addition, he became secretary to the Grand Prix meeting, the person to whom Stanley Barnes (as Clerk of the Course) and all the other RAC officials were to report. He was not, perhaps, the ideal choice, as persuading Samuelson to take an initiative was said to be 'like pushing a ton of lead uphill'.

With the word out that 'the buck stops with Geoffrey', the anxious Samuelson had initiative enough to enlist the best of allies, Lord Howe, and Howe at once formed and led a talented and experienced Grand Prix sub-committee. The choice of his fellow Old Etonian, Lord Waleran, as Vice-Chairman might, in more modern times, have aroused cries of cronyism, but the forty-three-year-old Waleran proved highly useful, for he was an influential figure in London society with the ability to melt the fiercest opposition during a weekend at his Gatsby-esque country house in Devon. Waleran had competed before the war in the Monte Carlo Rally and at Brooklands and Le Mans; he had been a courageous Wing Commander, mentioned in wartime dispatches, and he was now hoping to enter the Grand Prix as co-driver of a friend's elderly Talbot. Other notable members of Howe's sub-committee were the Brooklands stalwart Maj.-Gen. Loughborough (winner in 1932 of the

Above and opposite: The aerodrome's old heartland, as seen in the mid-1960s. A former store for anti-gas equipment and a latrine survive in front of the hangar. The roadway in the foreground (*above*) must be 'the concrete leading to the grandstand area', where a sole official attempted to create order out of chaos. (*BRDC Archive*)

first RAC Rally); Fred Craner (who had almost run pre-war Donington Park single-handed); John Morgan (secretary of the Junior Car Club and a former Clerk of Course at Brooklands and Donington); Sammy Davis (Sports Editor of *The Autocar*, one of the original 'Bentley Boys'); Desmond Scannell (secretary of the British Racing Drivers' Club); Rodney Walkerley (Sports Editor of *The Motor*) and the distinguished sports car driver 'TASO' Mathieson. All Howe's sub-committee members would subsequently assist in some important capacity at the meeting except 'TASO', but then he had only recently settled in France, newly married to a glamorous film star.

With his sub-committee fully operational, Howe kept regularly in touch with Wilfrid Andrews and Geoffrey Samuelson. He also consulted leading British drivers, most notably the three who were full members of the RAC: the Ansell cousins, Bob and Geoff (owners of a pre-war Maserati and ERA) and Leslie Johnson (who had recently bought the ERA company and was hoping to make the E-type ERA fully competitive).

One of Howe's earliest successes at Pall Mall had been to persuade the chairman that there should be a supporting race for 500cc cars. The growing interest in these small, home-made machines, he explained, was one of the country's success stories. To foster the 500s would redound to the credit of the RAC. It was a brilliant concept, exactly right for the times. Penny-pinching regulations! Tiny engines! Exciting power-to-weight ratios! Stimulation for inventive thinking by the engineers of tomorrow! The 500s did, of course, still cause some amusement. Even one of their biggest supporters, journalist Gregor Grant, wrote of 'the Skimpy-Whatnot, built entirely from tenth-hand bits in Harold Overdraft's backyard'. There were some eccentric

designs and odd-sounding names, like Buzzie, Imp, Tiger Kitten and Spink Squanderbug.

Professional constructors were just coming in and looking as if they would soon take over from the amateurs with their Skimpy-Whatnots, though the Marwyn company offered a somewhat suspect design. Lord Strathcarron, who was currently campaigning a Marwyn, had told lurid stories about its handling, and another driver, less lucky than Strathcarron, had recently

Above: The farm as it was in 1948. (*Graham Churchill*)

Opposite: The airfield circuit at the time the Grand Prix was first announced.

START

been killed testing one. The Cooper company looked a much better bet. A Surbiton garage owner, Charles Cooper, and his son, John, had just made a model available for customers. It was not cheap, at around £500, but a talented eighteen-year-old called Stirling Moss was already making news in one at the major hill-climbs. Howe's enthusiasm was infectious and Andrews had quickly agreed to a race for 500s.

As the sub-committee made progress on the big issues, Geoffrey Samuelson attended with meticulous care and courtesy to the minutiae of his steadily proliferating incoming mail. On just one August day, for example, not only was the Abington Brewery of Northampton offering to supply him with kegs of beer, but he also received offers from Campbell Praed of Wellingborough and Ind Coope & Allsopp's of Burton-on-Trent. Meanwhile, the Home Farm at Silverstone joined the list of those offering him milk; and Barclay's Bank at Brackley would obligingly look after his takings.

One job left to a surprisingly late resolution was that of the medical provision. The St John's Ambulance Brigade was eventually signed up in September (at a cost of £52 10s 0d) and, only two weeks before the race, Samuelson finally secured a Chief Medical Officer: 'Just a line to confirm our telephone conversation this morning,' he wrote to the Towcester doctor Frederick Gowland Hopkins, 'and to thank you most sincerely on behalf of the club in accepting the post of Hon. Medical Officer for the Grand Prix race…' 'Hoppy' Hopkins, whose sister (Jacquetta Hawkes) married J. B. Priestley and whose father had received the Nobel Prize for discovering vitamins, soon acquired enthusiastic helpers like Dr 'Frosty' Winterbottom. Their duties, it seems, were not completely full-time: 'Providing you can

fix it with your arrangements,' wrote Samuelson to Hopkins, 'it would be of the greatest assistance if you could attend on Thursday and Friday during part of the hours of practice.'

Samuelson was very late finalising arrangements for the refreshments and licensed bars, the contract for the catering eventually going to the Birmingham firm of Pattison-Hughes, with whose representative, a Mr Bazley, Samuelson held an urgent late discussion in the aerodrome's control tower. Samuelson hated making a fuss. Told to ensure that the catering in the Members' Enclosure was absolutely first-class, he gently wrote to Bazley: 'Should you see your way to make it possible, perhaps some extra enticement might be used there.'

The grandstand to be erected by the start-line had been sold out within a week of its announcement, so a second was ordered. By 31 August, the RAC had received £1,084 10s 0d in advance grandstand ticket and car park sales. A month later, as the race drew nearer, Geoffrey Samuelson found himself under increasing pressure to supply tickets to friends. 'Very sorry,' he replied to one acquaintance, 'I can't manage to find a spare seat to send you free, as I would have liked, but as the area is comparatively small and the demand very great, I am now in considerable difficulty. Incidentally, the grandstand is opposite the pits, if that interests you.' By the end of September this second grandstand was also full, and nearly £10,000 had been taken altogether in advanced sales.

* * *

Jimmy Brown, from his new HQ in the old guardhouse, resourcefully masterminded a tightly budgeted renaissance of the airfield. Each day, teams of local ladies collected brooms, bowls, paper towels, soap and disinfectant from him as they began cleaning out the most strategically placed of the derelict buildings. Beds were installed in the cleaned huts for scaffolders and other full-time workers needed at the site. The ladies also formed lines to sweep the overgrown runways.

Smith Churchill at Luffield Abbey Farm, meanwhile, was proving helpful, allowing several barns to be cleared out for the use of race officials. A former cowshed was earmarked for Maj. Dixon-Spain's Race Control, and a potato store for the telephone exchange. It was amazing what a quick coat of paint could achieve. Churchill's brother gallantly drove his tractor all the way from Norfolk to help shift the 170 tons of straw bales that would define the circuit and give spectators a sense of protection. Churchill's employers, the Bucks Agricultural Committee, were paid £82 10s 0d for the temporary use of their workers in racetrack preparation. And the RAC paid them a further £9 12s 0d for 'bales of straw and mowing grass'.

Brown made value-for-money deals with many local firms. Alcock's of Brackley, for example, received £150 13s 0d for general work on the track (in addition to £327 15s 7d for fences), which included the many places on the runways where the constant touching-down of heavy bombers had destroyed the bituminous surface, exposing badly weathered concrete. There was also a seriously defective concrete joint running along the area where the Segrave and Seaman hairpin bends were to be created.

National firms were used for the biggest jobs. Scaffolding Ltd created the grandstands, pits and footbridge (for £1,419 5s 0d); Johns & Sons (for £442 15s 0d) provided the marquees, plus further fencing and screens for the holes in the ground that served, most unsatisfactorily, as lavatories (there was no running water). The Antone Company provided the PA system (£120); Coventry Telephones (£36 19s 7d) and the East Midland Electricity Board (£49 1s 0d) helped alleviate other basic inadequacies; and the Towcester Town Council measured the track (£6 8s 4d), establishing the official distance of 3.67 miles.

As the first of the two days of practice approached, Jimmy Brown was under great pressure. Though the scaffolding was now up for both the grandstands, the canvas roofs had not yet materialised. There were delays, too, in the agricultural wire fencing needed to define key areas like the back of the pits, and the footbridge's foundations were awaiting cement. Amid all the considerable confusion, some contractors' vehicles carelessly ran over the white paint at the starting grid when it was still wet, and, much to Jimmy Brown's displeasure, casual motorists kept calling in to take a look round. Areas of responsibility between the circuit management and the RAC seemed blurred. Telephone wires between the two places were regularly buzzing. Brown, if angry, tended to become more Scottish, and when he finally lost his temper with Samuelson, telling him that, in the event of any future race meetings, all the contractors should work entirely through him at the circuit with properly worded contracts, he sounded like Rob Roy.

The RAC's beautifully kept financial ledger abounded in urgent last-minute purchases: armlets (£6 9s 4d and £11 7s 5d); victory wreaths (£10); flags (£53 14s 0d); a scoring board (£12 10s 0d); and a booth (£8 15s 3d) to house the timekeepers by the start-line. The pages for expenses continued to outstrip those for income.

CHAPTER 4

The thirty-nine-year-old Gigi Villoresi, like Chiron, enjoyed the good things in life. Only a few days earlier, during the race weekend at Florence, he had found time to hire a horse-drawn carriage with Raymond Sommer to go up into the hills of Fiesole for dinner. The race itself, for Formula 2 cars, had been a miserable affair, marred by the death and injury of several spectators, so Gigi was pleased for the diversion of a three-day drive to England with his friend and protégé, Alberto Ascari.

They'd said their goodbyes in Milan to Gigi's mother and Alberto's wife. Gigi's Lancia Aprilia was now heading for the Great St Bernard as fast as the poor conditions allowed, taking the same route as their Maseratis that had left in a lorry a day earlier with the dependable Guarino Bertocchi in charge. A clear piece of road at last allowed Gigi to open up the throttle. He smiled contentedly. Speed was among the good things in life.

* * *

Raymond Mays' new MK VI Bentley had left Lincolnshire in its dusty wake. 'The racing game,' he once wrote, 'tends to foster an unrelenting attitude towards a piece of machinery!' He was heading for the Welcombe Hotel outside Stratford-upon-Avon. For Mays, a fine hotel was part of the pleasure of going motor racing and the Welcombe fitted his preference for a country house atmosphere.

Left: Luigi Villoresi.

Opposite: With Alberto Ascari on a later visit to Silverstone. (*John Pearson*)

He knew Northampton was out of the question. The foreign drivers had been booked in at Northampton's two best hotels, the Angel and the Grand. The more affluent British drivers would probably be there, too. Meanwhile the RAC had block-booked for its army of officials the Plough and Cornhill hotels, as well as Brackley's Ye Olde Crowne. The cheap hotels, like Foxton's Commercial, would be full of patrolmen.

Mays tended to keep apart from the unsophisticated horse-play that accompanied race meetings. There would be fun for the next three nights at most of the nearby hotels and pubs. When the British drivers had gone across to Holland to help open the Zandvoort circuit that summer, Duncan Hamilton and Tony Rolt (after some excitement with a live eel in a restaurant) had imaginatively eluded pursuit by the police by driving Gordon Watson's jeep into their hotel foyer. Peter Walker and Leslie Brooke were equally high-spirited, Walker known to introduce chickens from his farm into classy restaurants, Brooke, who had no fear of heights, to shin up hotel drainpipes and balance decorously outside bedroom windows. Mays preferred a more sophisticated brand of fun with a small coterie of friends at hotels like the Welcombe.

With bushy hair surrounding a bald dome, Mays looked more like an eccentric academic than a conventional racing driver. His immaculate dress sense brought an unusual sartorial distinction to the paddocks. In his easy affability, he had a touch of the theatre matinée idol, and Mays had, indeed, once been an enthusiastic amateur actor. Like his contemporary Louis Chiron, he still enjoyed being centre stage. At the same time, he was a private person, as detached as he was charming, someone few people could really get to know.

May's current BRM project – British Racing Motors' publicly funded Grand Prix car that was expected to put the country back on terms with the leading continentals – had ensured he stayed a household name. His private life, meanwhile, continued to be a quiet source of gossip. Despite his schooldays at Oundle and his time in the Guards, was he quite the gentleman he affected to

Above: Raymond Mays' home, Eastgate House, Bourne, Lincs. (*John Pearson*)

Opposite: Raymond Mays at home, with a photograph of a favourite actress (Phyllis Dare) and paintings by Gordon Crosby. (*John Pearson*)

be? He talked of the family wool business, but hadn't his father owned a tannery and a slaughter house? And wasn't he also into fertilizers? A further topic of interest was Mays' mother, Annie, presiding protectively over their home, Eastgate House, Bourne.

Once, it was said, when a new ERA was being prepared for her son, Annie had suddenly appeared in the Eastgate workshops brandishing a pistol. 'You take care of building that car!' she cried to the mechanics. 'If ever anything happens to my Raymond, I'll shoot you all dead!' Mays' long-serving chief mechanic, 'Tinker' Richardson, had been there at the time. 'We believed her, too. She adored him. And he absolutely worshipped her.' Another crisis occurred when their handsome young lodger, Peter Berthon, a ladies' man to whom both mother and son were equally devoted, suddenly announced he was getting married. The furious Annie at once dubbed his glamorous bride 'The Terrible Turk'. Worse, she set to with scissors, cutting off the sleeves of his shirts and the legs of his trousers, before throwing his possessions, gramophone and all, out of a first-floor window.

Mays was discreet about his homosexuality and, for all the ambiguities surrounding him, he was very widely respected and liked. On form, he could be a great entertainer. He was a genuine patriot showing messianic zeal towards the promotion of British motor sport. And his ability to elicit sponsorship from the trade had, all along, been ground-breaking in its aspirations and achievements.

Although he was now forty-nine, *The Autocar* had placed him first in its Top 12 drivers of 1948 and he had just won the British hill-climb championship for the second successive time. But he had retired in the only three road races he had entered this year. His racing career was nearing its end, and he knew his twelve-year-old ERA would be outclassed at the Grand Prix. He had to be at Silverstone, however, to keep his name before the public, but it was hard to focus on the race, preoccupied as he was with current BRM difficulties.

One of Mays' anxieties was Peter Berthon, his chief designer. It was beginning to seem as if his trust in his long-term associate might be ill placed. Ten months ago, at the launch at Claridge's, Berthon had suggested the BRM would be race-worthy this year. But, as Mays had had to admit recently, the engine had not yet been tested and the car's trials would start 'early next year'. *Motor Sport* was pressing Mays to say more. 'Cannot a hint be given as to why the first car has been delayed? A progress report would do much to guarantee the continued enthusiasm that exists for this vital undertaking. We invite Raymond Mays to submit it.' He was not going to do so. The miscalculations would be too apparent. There would be questions asked at Silverstone, for sure, but the silver-tongued Mays would find a way around them. And, in the meanwhile, determined to reach Stratford-upon-Avon in good time for dinner, he suppressed his many anxieties and drove on as unrelentingly as ever.

* * *

Gigi Villoresi was guiding the Lancia through the Alps with all the assurance of someone who had raced in fifty Grands Prix. He had first met Ascari, nine years his junior, in 1940, when Ascari, who had just competed in his first car race (the Mille Miglia), approached Villoresi about a single-seater he was selling. Gigi, knowing it was a poor car, sold him instead a Maserati 6CL for a bargain price of 12,000 lire. He also, quite remarkably, managed to organise an entry for Ascari in the Tripoli Grand Prix of 1940 (in which he himself was driving the latest 4CL Maserati). He came fourth and Ascari, in only his second race, an impressive ninth. Two weeks later they were both back in Italy, competing in the Targa Florio, held in a Palermo park. Villoresi won but Ascari hit a tree, badly damaging the Maserati. Eighteen days later Italy entered the Second World War on the side of the Germans.

The conversation in Gigi's Lancia naturally turned to England. Ascari hadn't been there before; his mentor knew it well. In 1938 at the Donington Grand Prix, Gigi, in the latest eight-cylinder Maserati, had upheld Italian honour against Mercedes and Auto Union. Later that summer, he had raced a Maserati 6CM at Crystal Palace, an expedition he was fond of recalling: 'England is wonderful. Mind you, it always rains there. Dear Carlo Maltempi was with me that visit. We had some free days before the Crystal Palace meeting, so we bought umbrellas and macs and became tourists. We shopped and shopped and then, in a fit of economy, got a bus instead of a taxi. One of those strange double-deckers. I led the way up the stairs, Carletto following. Then the driver slammed on his brakes, I lost my balance, fell on top of Carletto, and we and all our parcels, bursting open, went tumbling down, ending up on top of a poor old lady. She took it rather well. That's England for you.'

Travelling cheerfully together towards the Grand Prix, Villoresi and Ascari might have been taken for brothers, and that, in effect, is what they were. They had met only a year after Gigi's younger brother Emilio, a promising racing driver four years his junior, had been killed at Monza testing a Scuderia Ferrari Alfa Romeo. Soon the two families were the best of friends and Alberto found himself in the role of the younger brother Gigi had lost. The relationship was further strengthened when, during the war, Alberto married Emilio Villoresi's former girlfriend, Mietta.

Alberto had spent 1946 building up the family car business in Milan and growing fat on Mietta's pasta. In 1947, however, Gigi had persuaded him (though still a novice with only three races to his name) to compete with him at the highest level, and it was soon clear that Alberto had all of his father Antonio's talent. He had already won the San Remo Grand Prix in 1948, and perhaps, in this his twentieth motor race, he would win at Silverstone...

* * *

As Prince Bira drove up the A5 in his latest drophead coupé, there were partial regrets that he had not flown up from Cornwall in his latest toy, his Miles Gemini. But this solitary drive from his London flat suited his current sombre mood. Bira wasn't usually given to dark introspection. At thirty-four, he could look back on a delightful life that had been one long succession of wonderful treats, each treat being that much more delicious than its predecessor; a life, too, abounding in excitement and happily cocooned from unhappiness by all that money and privilege could bring.

He had been born Prince Birabongse Bhanudej Bhanubandh, the grandson of the King of Siam. On the death of his parents he had been brought up as an English gentleman by his cousin and guardian, Prince Chula. Six years older than Bira and even richer, Chula was completely under Bira's spell, indulging the young prince's every whim, an Eton education being followed by some tuition in sculpture from Charles Wheeler and much motor racing at Brooklands. A photograph of 1935 shows Bira and Chula posing with their current collection of cars strung across the track: an ERA, MG Magnette and Riley Imp, together with seven road cars including an Aston Martin, a Rolls-Royce and a Bentley.

The ERA (named Romulus) had been Bira's twenty-first birthday present from Chula. A party had been held at Wheeler's studio with a hired dance band, food sent in from the Berkeley Hotel, and – because Bira and Chula both adored ballet – the whole of Col. de Basil's Russian company, currently appearing in London, in attendance. At midnight the guest of honour, the new ERA, was wheeled in, accompanied by a smiling Raymond Mays and Peter Berthon. Leonide Massine later partnered Alexandra Danilova and Tamara Toumanova as part of an impromptu cabaret. Bira was never backwards in his birthday requests. He had gone to see Mays at Bourne before floating the idea of such a present.

Chula not only continued to ensure that Bira always had the best of everything – by the late 1930s Bira had a choice of a Maserati and 3 ERAs – but also turned himself into one of the finest team managers in the business. Chula's money and organisational skills helped mastermind famous victories like the 'light car' race at Monaco in 1936, in which Bira's competitors included Howe and Villoresi.

Bira loved flying and, when war came, he had hoped to join the RAF, but because of the neutral status of Thailand (as Siam had recently become) he had difficulty even in joining the home guard. They had spent the war largely at Tredethy, the large house Chula had acquired in Cornwall for himself, Bira and their young wives, where the two cousins would daily discuss and dream of peace and further motor racing. Chula, moreover, wrote books about their pre-war exploits that kept Bira's fame to the fore.

But somehow things after the war weren't quite the same. Bira had suddenly grown up. And now he had broken with Chula altogether. When Bira had begun racing, he'd painted a small white mouse on his cars to show his thanks to Chula, whose nickname was 'Nou', Siamese for little mouse. Their garage housing the cars in London had become known as the White Mouse Garage. But now the White Mouse team was no more. Bira needed his space. He loved Chula, despite all the tantrums, and felt immensely grateful to him. But at thirty-four, he had to make his own way.

Motor racing was also changing, becoming a little more professional. Bira was already a contracted works driver for Simca in Formula 2 along with Sommer and Wimille. Chula hadn't liked that. Bira had also had discussions with Enzo Ferrari. Chula had tried hard to acquire the latest Grand Prix Alfa Romeo for 1948, perhaps as a last throw to keep the White Mouse team alive, but Alfa wouldn't sell to a privateer. Instead, a deal had been done with Maserati for their very latest 4CLT. Bira hadn't seen the car yet, but the dependable chief mechanic Stanley Holgate had collected it and would be bringing it up to Silverstone. It was Chula's final gift. He was also allowing Bira to keep his 4CL. But he had taken Romulus back, and that hurt.

In Chula's absence, Bira's English wife, the Princess Ceril, was doing all the paperwork. She had always been good at keeping an accurate lap-chart. But she, like Chula, didn't understand his need for space. Ceril had acted too possessively at Florence and the subsequent row meant she wouldn't be at Silverstone. At least for one race meeting there'd be no problems over the pretty girls who were somehow always there with their siren eyes.

Bira (*right*) chatting to Bob Gerard at a later Silverstone meeting. (*John Pearson*)

His destination, Stony Stratford, could not be far away, and there his young friend, Tony Rudd, would be sorting out the accommodation arrangements. But thoughts of Ceril wouldn't go away. She was so devoted, like Chula; she loved him still, despite everything, but he couldn't breathe and their ten-year marriage looked to be nearing its end. How hard he had tried to make it a good summer! They'd flown to Nice in the Miles Gemini and stayed at the Hôtel de Paris for the Monaco race. They'd met King George VI at a garden party at Buckingham Palace and attended the Eton-Harrow cricket match at Lord's. On Lake Garda, which she loved, they'd enjoyed both the yacht and the Maserati coupé he'd bought there. She was currently looking for a house on the lake.

But now there would be no more parties with Chula at Tredethy. No more White Mouse Racing. And probably no more Ceril. A new life was dawning. Freer and less cocooned. It was what he wanted. And what he wanted he always got. He was beginning this new life with the very latest and much-coveted Maserati. Yet it was with a strangely heavy heart that he applied the brakes and slowed a little on entering Stony Stratford.

* * *

The Lancia Aprilia had left Berne well behind, and, with it, unhappy memories of the tragic Grand Prix at Bremgarten. The dangers of the sport never worried Gigi. He accepted its terms unconditionally. 'If you're fearful,' he would say, 'don't even think of beginning.' Nonetheless, the death of a friend like Achille Varzi was a deep distress. Only that winter they had enjoyed great times together on the ship taking them to races in South America. Achille was a difficult man with strong opinions. But he was also *un grande signore*, someone very special.

With Alberto at the wheel, Luigi was able to relax and admire the expertise with which each obstacle to progress was handled. How strange that they were such good friends and yet such opposites – Alberto, dark and swarthy; he himself, blue-eyed and silver-haired. Emotionally too. Gigi knew his own greatest weakness was his impetuosity and inability to dissemble. His face, his friends declared, could always be read like a book. But with dear Alberto it was so different. He kept most of his thoughts carefully locked up. They shared one important thing, however – their prosperous Milan families. The Ascaris had long held an Alfa Romeo dealership in the Corso Sempione, extending over the whole of Lombardy. After Antonio Ascari's death (when Alberto was just seven years old), the dealership, taken over by an uncle, had continued to prosper. Gigi's own father, Gaetano Villoresi, had run a company that generated the city's electricity, and so he too had been brought up in handsome surroundings (in his case, the Corso Vercelli). His grandfather had been even more distinguished, an engineer who had built the important Canale Villoresi and whose name had also been perpetuated on a Milan street, the Via Eugenio Villoresi. But perhaps his great-grandfather was the most significant of all the early Villoresis? As a famous gardening expert, he had held a key position at Monza's villa and park. Monza! Gigi hadn't raced there since the death of Emilio. He and his poor widowed mother had had their share of tragedies. Not only had they lost Emilio but his brother Giuseppe had committed suicide.

And then there had been the horrors of war. Like most Italians they had been swept along by fascism in the 1930s. Gigi had loved the warm reception he always had received on his regular visits to Tripoli in the heart of Italian Africa, often being looked after personally by Mussolini's deputy, Italo Balbo, the Governor of Libya. Like most of his friends, he accepted Italian imperialism. Count 'Johnny' Lurani had even given up racing in 1935 to serve in the Ethiopian War.

Mussolini's pact with Hitler had come as a shock; so, too, had the onset of war. Gigi and Alberto had joined in converting the Ascari garage into an engineering works, and soon they were not only building and maintaining military vehicles but also supplying the Italian army with petrol via exciting tanker runs. Alberto had preferred to stay at home (but, then, he was courting Mietta) so Gigi alone had enjoyed the thrill of leading great motorised cavalcades from Tripoli into the deserts beyond. It was fun at first, an alternative to the excitement on the track, now denied him. There had been the occasional setback, like the day his ship capsized off Tripoli harbour. There he was, floating helplessly in the water, blowing a whistle – for some reason they'd all been issued with emergency whistles – and hoping some kind boatman would come along and pick him up. Then, in 1943, came his capture in the desert. And the less than amusing aftermath. He would never discuss the war these days, not even with Alberto.

Alberto's handling of the Aprilia was deft, so quick and neat. Yet he knew that he himself was the quicker, on both open and closed roads. Experience counted. But might the pupil one day overtake the teacher? He was still very much the number one, the current Italian champion. Alberto had only won at San Remo after he himself had suffered problems. But at Silverstone?

* * *

Reg Parnell, driving down with his family from Derby in his SS Jaguar, had just joined the A50 from the A6. A short,

Reg Parnell, by Ralph Sallon. (*Motor-Racing Past and Present, BP/Shellmex, 1956*)

stocky man with receding fair hair, at thirty-seven Parnell was Britain's leading racing driver, having triumphed over the many difficulties his working-class background imposed.

Parnell's parents had run a pub in Derby. He had left school early to help his elder brother in a haulage business started in the pub's backyard, so by his early teens he was driving lorries and charabancs and already developing into a capable mechanic. In due course, he became a partner in the prospering business and, in 1935, at the age of twenty-four, he was able to buy his first racing car, a single-seater MG in which he was soon making a name for speed and recklessness at Donington and Brooklands. In 1937, he lost control near the top of the Brooklands banking and slid down into Kay Petre's single-seater Austin, which overturned and flung her out. One of the best and most popular lady drivers of the day, she eventually recovered from her serious injuries, but the RAC took away Reg's competition licence, only restoring it in 1939. Realising it was better not to alienate the establishment further, Reg made a fulsome public apology.

The family haulage business, requisitioned by the government in the war, proved extremely lucrative. Not only did Reg's lorries ferry vital supplies all over the country, but also, on the side, helped gather together large numbers of unwanted racing cars in Derby, purchased on the cheap. He was assisted in this by two friends who also nursed ambitions as racing drivers, the brothers Joe and Fred Ashmore. It was a cloak and dagger operation. Lorries would bring in their booty at night, concealed under wraps, and over thirty high-quality racing cars with large quantities of spares were eventually stored away in barns and sheds. Unwanted Bentleys and other luxury cars also rapidly multiplied. The operation constantly grew until anything mechanical that might later offer a good profit was bought up and stored. Unwanted transporters were converted to ambulances and sold to the Army. At the end of the war, prices satisfactorily rocketed and Reg made a fortune.

He was also instrumental in helping many people back into motor sport. As he drove down to Northampton, Parnell had the satisfaction of knowing that nearly half the cars on the Grand Prix grid had passed through his hands. Like Raymond Mays, albeit in a very different way, Reg Parnell played an important part in the post-war recovery of the British racing fraternity.

From 1946, he was in a position to race very seriously, helped by a joint venture with the Ashmores – the founding of Highfield Garages in Derby, where their own cars were prepared alongside those of many customers. With the highly experienced Wilkie Wilkinson brought in as Works Manager, Highfield flourished. Reg also became a farmer with a prestigious estate, complete with old country house, just outside Derby. There were a number of prosperous farmers from privileged backgrounds among the top drivers. Peter Walker, Peter Whitehead, John Bolster and Geoffrey Ansell were typical. Now Reg, in resourcefully overcoming his distinctly less privileged background, was one of them.

With the best available equipment at his disposal, he prospered in the immediate post-war period both at home and abroad, twice winning the BRDC's Gold Star. He knew how to handle top-class machinery. That summer, he'd done a secret deal with Count 'Johnny' Lurani and the Ambrosiana people for a brand new 4CLT Maserati that he had collected in Italy and raced in pouring rain at Turin's Valentino Park, where he came fifth in the Grand Prix. And two weeks ago, at the opening of Goodwood, he'd won the five-lap Formula Libre race, albeit against modest opposition. He knew his Maserati wasn't fully sorted yet. Nonetheless, he fancied his chances at Silverstone.

* * *

Villoresi and Ascari were held up at the Swiss-French border. Delays at customs posts, where war-induced xenophobia still lurked, were currently the norm, and an unusual car like the Villoresi Lancia naturally aroused extra interest. Word might also have been out that the Scuderia Ambrosiana needed careful watching. Benefiting from a name that commemorated Milan's patron saint, they had become experts in the wheeling and dealing that was

necessary to circumvent stringent post-war currency restrictions. The deal they had recently done with Reg's friend Leslie Brooke may also have had repercussions. Brooke, like Parnell, had come

Below and inset: Racing on public roads was the norm everywhere but England in the early post-war years. Gordon Watson, seen competing in the Ulster Trophy at Ballyclare, 1947 (which he led before crashing), typifies the challenge of those years. (*Marjorie Watson*)

across to the continent to pick up a new Maserati, which he had raced at both Albi and Turin. But when en route to Silverstone, it had been impounded by the Italian customs, seizing upon some irregularity in the Ambrosiana paperwork.

Alberto's passport, too, had enough stamps on it to preoccupy suspiciously inclined minds. During the war, he had not only honeymooned in Switzerland but also mysteriously returned there several times for long periods when his relationship with the Nazis in Milan became uneasy after the Italian surrender.

There was a certain amount of mystery about Alberto's Silverstone entry. He and Gigi had been campaigning the Maseratis under the Ambrosiana banner all season and yet his entry had been such a late one there was no mention of him in the Silverstone programme and he was given the race number allotted to the non-appearing Farina. Perhaps this had nothing to do with delicate Ambrosiana strategies, but such suspicions were understandable. (When Fred Ashmore acquired Ascari's Ambrosiana Maserati in 1949, the deal was done in an ice cream parlour.)

Eventually, after a long wait, the two friends' paperwork was found to be completely in order and the Aprilia moved onwards. The delay, though irritating, was not too worrying. All Gigi and Alberto had to do was to arrive in time for the second day's practice…

CHAPTER 5

The organisers were lucky. It was dull but dry on the morning of Thursday 30 September, the first day of practice. A few resourceful enthusiasts, who had somehow managed to get off work and overcome petrol rationing or the lack of transport at Silverstone's nearest railway stations, were directed into Enclosure B on the outside of Woodcote on the payment of 5s. 'Enclosure', however, was a relative term and they were soon investigating the 500s' paddock, situated between the entrance road and Enclosure B, and walking delightedly down the track to examine the Grand Prix pits.

There they learnt the disappointing news that the Alfa Romeos would not be coming. Nor, too, the Ferraris, despite 'a voluminous interchange of cables between the RAC and Giuseppe Farina and Raymond Sommer'. The motoring press were to give Alfa a hard time. 'In marked contrast to the large number of British drivers who have raced in Europe since the end of the war entirely at their own expense,' commented *The Motor*, 'this great Italian manufacturing concern would appear to have no wish to make an appearance unless the terms are entirely in their favour.' With Monza only two weeks away and air travel prohibitively expensive, it was a harsh judgment.

There was much excitement at the arrival of each Grand Prix team, sweeping past the pits and turning left at the footbridge into the main paddock area near the farm. All foreign vehicles were a rarity, so Bill Boddy felt it worth noting that Philippe Étancelin had arrived in a small Renault saloon, that one of the Lago-Talbots had been towed behind a Peugeot 202, another carried by an open Mercedes diesel, and a third by a modern Chevrolet lorry. British participants also added to the sense of exoticism. Reg Parnell's red Maserati was towed in by a stylish Riley Gamecock. Bira's similar Maserati was brought in by a Hudson 'Utility' Coupé, from the back of which, like magicians, the mechanics slid out a huge steel working bench.

The paddock was soon exuding a growing conviviality, centred around the buffet bar in a marquee behind the pits, though most teams were well provided with their own supplies of strong refreshment. (The Ferodo caravan was said to be highly unusual in its inability to provide callers with anything stronger than a cup of tea.) Peter Walker and John Bolster were just two of many drivers who liked to have a flask of spirits to hand in the pits.

* * *

The 500s were expecting a two-hour practice session beginning at 11.00 a.m., but the track was not ready so it was delayed and reduced to one hour. Lord Howe and his Clerk of the Course, Col. Barnes, were much in evidence, motoring around the circuit to the various problem areas. Howe's Type 57S Bugatti (in his old racing colours of black and dark blue) was a chic two-seater coupé, the ultimate in late 1930s road-holding, Atalante body-styling and comfort. Col. Barnes, in contrast, drove a 1948 Healey Westland Roadster.

Eventually, all was made ready and Howe and Barnes began one final lap of reconnaissance. For Howe it was a special moment. A modest man, he might well have opened the course on race day, but instead had asked his good friend John Cobb to do so, as current holder of the world's land speed record. This, then, was his own quiet moment of celebration, as a pack of racing cars was about to be officially unleashed at Silverstone for the very first time.

With the lap of reconnaissance over and the last of the errant spectators sent back from the pits to Enclosure B, a motley collection of 500s emerged, not so much in a pack as in desultory ones and twos. The fragile machines looked particularly tiny on the wide expanses of aerodrome tarmac. A smell of hot engines and clutch plates was soon in the air. For some, just the act of getting out on to the track before the end of the session was a challenge. Ken Smith's home-built special, for example, had vibrated so much that it had broken its chassis in two. After a hastily improvised welding job, Smith cleared scrutineering and rushed out just in time to complete one tentative lap. Vibration was a problem common to all 500s. Lord Strathcarron described sitting in his Marwyn, with its

single-cylinder high-compression engine only inches from his back, as 'a continual vibro massage'.

By the end of practice, the Coopers had proved as dominant as expected. Stirling Moss, lapping in his cream-coloured car in 3 minutes 17.4 seconds, was a whole 10 seconds faster than his

Above: Bob Ansell (*second from left*) chats to George Bainbridge (*back to camera*) and the injured Peter Whitehead (*left*) in the pits beside his Maserati.

Opposite: Bolster's ERA (Remus) at Zandvoort, 1948, with John Bolster (*left*), entrant Peter Bell (*centre back*) and chief mechanic George Boyle (*right*). (*John Pearson*)

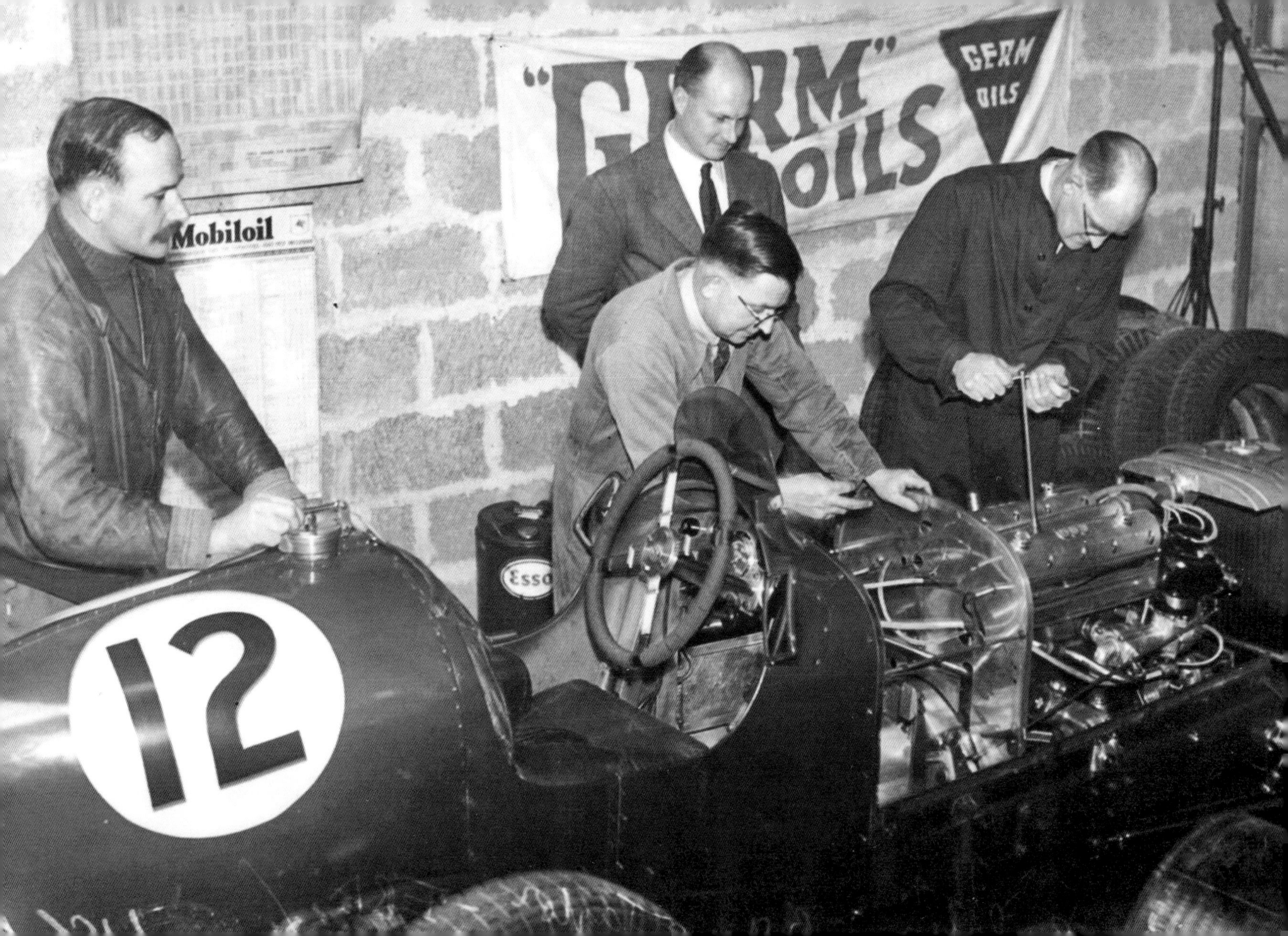
Mobiloil
"GERM" OILS
GERM OILS
Esso
12

nearest rival, a young Lancashire stockbroker, Robert Coward. Twenty-five-year-old John Cooper, driving the works machine, was fourth fastest. There were four Coopers in the top six.

Robert Coward was a very typical 500 participant. He had teamed up with a friend and fellow novice, architect Geoff Lang, to build a racing car at weekends. After fourteen months of work with a Fiat chassis, brakes, wheels, springing and steering, their 'Cowlan' eventually emerged at a total cost of £12 10s 0d. To their amazement, the car did the standing quarter-mile at a local aerodrome in 18 seconds on its very first test. 'We were tickled to bits.' Reg Phillips, a Sheffield trials driver who had been inspired by the RAC's announcement of the Silverstone meeting to build a 500, had used a pre-war Austin 7 chassis. During practice, a fractured gearbox support member had to be welded. Then the Girling brakes proved more powerful than he'd anticipated. 'I was haring down Hangar Straight at about 75 mph, slung on the anchors, and my front wheels locked solid. Something had to go and in this case it was the axle, the ends of which twisted right over. Rotten shame.'

Howe watched the practice session indulgently. As Patron of the 500 Club (with Raymond Mays as his Vice-Patron), he was delighted that there were now nearly 600 members. He saw the 500s as the only available way forward to challenge the old continental supremacy in motor racing. The continentals, with their plethora of road races, were currently well ahead of the British, as they had nearly always been. Others might scoff at the unreliability of the little machines and their speedway engines. Howe knew better. Though Saturday's Grand Prix was of great importance to the future of British motor sport, in his eyes the 500s held almost equal significance.

* * *

The Lancia had been finding the French *Routes Nationales* to its taste, and would reach the English Channel by evening, but Gigi was no longer hopeful of making second practice. There had been too many roadworks in a battle-scarred country, too many priests on wobbly bikes, too many *garçons* playing *boule* on the verges, too many *camions* with fruit for the markets. His excellent knowledge of the roads to Reims just wouldn't be enough.

He would have loved to have made a detour to the public roads that formed the Reims-Gueux circuit. The Aprilia might have struggled on the two long straights, but it would have gone well through the villages. Last July's French Grand Prix had been significant for both Gigi and Alberto. For Gigi there had been an act of generosity that had allowed the ailing Tazio Nuvolari to take over the Maserati mid-race to see if he might still be well enough to compete. He wasn't. Poor Tazio had come in after a few quick laps, ashen white. For Alberto there had been the surprise of an Alfa Romeo drive when the team regrouped after Varzi's death. He had been anxious about accepting the Reims offer, but had distinguished himself, leading the race until required to let his team-mates through. The possibility of an Alfa Romeo contract had resulted, which Gigi, with his usual generosity, had urged his friend to take. But he didn't. He stayed with Maserati. He wouldn't say why.

But Gigi knew. The answer lay just 50 miles to the south of Reims: the circuit of Montlhéry. It was at the opening meeting of the Montlhéry autodrome, during the French Grand Prix of 1925, that Alberto's father had been killed, driving an Alfa Romeo. It was the one marque he had raced throughout his career. So the superstitious Alberto had turned down the offer.

Lord Selsdon's 1938 Talbot T26SS (shared with Lord Waleran) awaits scrutineering.

The sad but treasured memory of Antonio Ascari was a deep bond between them. Gigi at sixteen had sorrowfully watched the massive funeral cortège processing through the packed streets of Milan. The diminutive Alberto, a part of that procession, had later stood hand in hand with his father's chief mechanic, Giulio Ramponi, as his father was laid to rest amid the elaborate shrines of Milan's Monumental Cemetery. Gigi and Alberto had only recently returned there to gaze on Antonio's bronze bust...

* * *

All the Grand Prix traffic that had been entering the circuit during the 500's practice session had the frustration of having to wait at the end of the entrance road until they finished. This included Ecurie France's smart white Delahaye van bringing in Chiron's Lago-Talbot. It was no good Chiron angrily gesticulating across the track to the officials to let the late arrival across as soon as there was a gap in 500s approaching Woodcote. The RAC patrolmen

Leslie Johnson's E-type ERA (GP2) being worked on before first practice, when it was to have its moment of glory. (*Ferret Fotographics*)

Roy Salvadori's elderly Maserati being push-started on the first practice day as work begins on roofing the grandstand.

had been expressly forbidden by Col. Barnes to do such a thing. So there, facing the track, the Delahaye van stayed till the lunch break, to the admiration of many in Enclosure B. What an impressive array of spot lamps it possessed! And how neatly painted on the doors were all of Ecurie France's recent successes!

The Grand Prix cars came out for two hours' practice after the lunch break. Most of the journalists present subsequently ignored both days' practice sessions in their reports, but *Motor Sport's* Bill Boddy was the enthusiastic exception, rushing from corner to corner to take it all in. The cars, he noted, as they 'became warm and began to open up', raised 'a fair amount of dust' from the course. Through the dust he was alarmed to see how much the front wheels of Salvadori's Maserati and Gordon Watson's Alta 'flapped'. At Copse Corner Leslie Johnson 'held a slide' in the E-type ERA. Coming out of Woodcote, David Hampshire's old ERA passed Baring's old Maserati, which soon lost its taped-on number. There, too, 'the bottom of the tail of Brooke's aged ERA fell off' and Irishman Bobbie Baird's Emeryson passed by, smoking.

Boddy particularly liked the two hairpin bends at the central intersection, approached 'by those with passes along a delightful path':

Watching from Seaman Corner we saw Harrison's ERA spin round, Bolster shoot through the white tins which marked the course, Rosier rock his wheel as he cornered and Étancelin make his rear tyres smoke under acceleration. At Segrave Corner Bolster worked hard; Richardson's ERA-Riley slid appreciably, as did Walker's E-type ERA. Watson spun round in front of Rosier, Baird later doing the same thing in front of Johnson at Seaman Corner.

The experienced Comotti 'cornered beautifully'. From a distance, Boddy saw Étancelin's Talbot coming to a smoking halt on the exit from Copse. 'A nonchalant French mechanic came out to the car and Étancelin walked off through the stubble fields as a group of farm labourers gathered round the stricken Talbot.'

Back in the pits, Boddy was able to note that 'Mays suffered piston ring trouble after a few laps and rushed his ERA away in its van, the Emeryson caught fire, necessitating all-night work, and Peter Walker rode in on the tail of Ansell's Maserati, leaving the E-type ERA beside Seaman Straight!' Later, Boddy walked round the paddock, filling in on the various problems. Philippe Étancelin's propeller-shaft had come adrift, chewing up the floor. Fragments of his seat had been found sticking to the universal joint, so he had been very lucky to have emerged unscathed. Peter Walker's E-type, having broken its timing chain and damaged a rocker, was towed away, not to return. Chiron, who had only appeared at the end of the session, had been careful with his new car because of steering problems, but was confident they would be cured.

When Maj.-Gen. Loughborough's timekeepers finally put their findings together, there was encouraging news for home fans. Leslie Johnson had ended up with the fastest time of the day in his E-type ERA (GP2), having proved unexpectedly faster (2 58.6) than the Maseratis of Bira (2 59.6) and Parnell (2 59.8). The Herefordshire farmer Peter Walker was another British success, but though he was fourth fastest (2 59.8) in the other E-type ERA (GP1), it was out of the race and next day he would have to try to qualify a pre-war model.

By late afternoon, many of the Grand Prix drivers had disappeared to their hotels, intent on an evening's hilarity. Others, however, like John Bolster, who had forgotten to book a hotel and

Raymond Mays' ERA (R4D) at Becket's.

so had borrowed a caravan, stayed on to have their fun at the circuit. The escalating nocturnal merriment on the Thursday night at Silverstone took a predictable course. There were any number of cars to hand and, though it was dark, that only made the hairpin bends at the end of long straights more of a challenge. Jimmy Brown's precious straw bales and his 250 marker tubs were indeed a heady enticement to the party spirit. Playing dodgems had never been so good. News of the revelry eventually reached Bleak Hall Farm in Silverstone village, but there was nothing Jimmy Brown could do. The marshals and patrol men had long since gone, so he could only bury his head under the pillow and go back to sleep. Friday promised to be another busy day and, by the sound of it, there'd be a big clearing-up job in the morning.

There was, indeed. And, in all the circumstances, the memorandum that the furious Jimmy Brown later wrote Geoffrey Samuelson was remarkable for its restraint:

We need provision of guards – either Police or RAC – for the track during the nights of practice, to protect equipment and also prevent illegal use of the track by competitors or their associates. The drivers and their teams seem to think the track can be used at absolutely any time. We also need displayed a list of RAC rules so that would-be competitors or competitors' cars know that rules do exist whereby they are prevented from using the track, except on Practice Days or on RAC authority.

The Lago-Talbot of Philippe Étancelin (4) chases that of Louis Rosier (3) out of Seaman Corner during practice.

CHAPTER 6

Jimmy Brown was up early on the day of second practice, Friday 1 October, slightly mollified by the encouraging weather. Last-minute jobs included the provision of beds in Nissen huts for the car park attendants and other race-day helpers and the glueing of numbers along the seven rows of seats in each grandstand. While his wife Kay gallantly led teams putting up advertising hoardings and finishing roping off the spectator areas, he himself led others in salvaging hay bales and marker drums from the night's festivities.

As the paddock slowly filled, the disappointment that there was still no sign of Villoresi was tempered by the arrival of Bira's Maserati, changed from red to a dazzling royal blue after being resprayed overnight at Stony Stratford. (Gossip spread that Prince Chula had phoned Bira, threatening to take the car back unless it raced in Siamese colours.) And there was a new arrival, Toulo de Graffenried, whose 4CL had just been towed in behind a Lancia Aprilia. A glamorous young lady was soon neatly painting the No. 20 on the red Maserati that the Baron had regularly campaigned since its acquisition in the middle of 1947. Billy Boddy thought it looked 'rather rough', but the driver, in blue overalls, was 'tall, smart and smiling'. It was not long before a leak was discovered at the base of the petrol tank – just the start of a troublesome two days for de Graffenried.

Leaks seem to have been contagious, and all was not well with Raymond Mays' ERA as it neared Silverstone, returning from overnight repairs at Bourne. One of Mays' regular pre-war mechanics, Marshall Dorr, who was now running his own car-tuning firm in Northampton, happened to be nearing Silverstone, where he was to help out in the Mays pit, when he became aware of a strong smell of fuel. Minutes later, he passed an open lorry carrying Mays' ERA, from which fuel was pouring in a steady stream onto the road. So he stopped the lorry and did a quick repair job. When, just before 11.00 a.m., the Grand Prix cars were readied for their two hours of final practice, Mays' ERA was among them, full of fuel once again.

* * *

In the middle of the morning, Guy Scudamore Griffiths, a thirty-two-year-old motor dealer from Thames Ditton, left the fine collection of Alvises in his sales room near Paddington station and headed for Silverstone. Guy was also a photographer and on many Saturdays since the war he had recorded sprints, hill-climbs and races, subsequently selling his prints to the motoring press and individual drivers. He was the official photographer for *Road & Track*, and regularly featured in *Motor Sport* and *The Autocar*. His last job had been covering Goodwood's opening meeting.

He was returning to an area he had once known well, for Guy had been at Stowe School in the early 1930s, where Peter Whitehead had been one of his contemporaries. A Berkshire farmer who was also one of the most experienced of the British drivers, Whitehead would only be spectating at Silverstone as he was currently recovering from injuries in a crash at Croydon Airport. He was en route to Maranello to buy a Grand Prix Ferrari when his plane, on take-off, ended up in a private garden, killing the co-pilot and seriously injuring Peter and the two other passengers. A wealthy man, he currently owned the two ERAs that his cousin Peter Walker had at his disposal at Silverstone, and Guy was keen to hear all the latest gossip from the two Peters.

There was little traffic as Guy made his way up the A5 to Stony Stratford and then west along the A422. At the quiet market town of Buckingham, he joined a few other vehicles taking the narrow country lane to Dadford and Silverstone. There had been no aerodrome when he was at school. It had all been farmland. So it was with particular interest that he turned into the circuit. Almost at once he found his Citroën stopped at the tail of a long queue. An RAC patrolman saluted and courteously explained the hold-up: Grand Prix practice wasn't quite over. Until it stopped they couldn't get across to the paddock and infield. But it would be stopping soon, as it was almost one o'clock.

The familiar rasp of a pre-war ERA came and went, as the patrolman moved away to repeat his message. Guy had done some racing himself and was also an expert on engines, having worked for Napier in the war. Was that Peter's R10B? He walked up to the track to take a closer look.

* * *

The devoted Bill Boddy was already scribbling down key facts about the second practice session. Leslie Johnson had been absent, attending to business in the City. Duncan Hamilton had spun at Seaman Corner, and Brooke had scattered the marshals there. Sliding too wide, he had hit a marker tub, spun round three times, and been taken away, disconsolate, in a marshal's car. Murray charged the straw bales at Copse, damaging the steering, Gilbey's Maserati broke a piston, the engine being dismantled at the pits, and the Emeryson again caught fire. Geoffrey Ansell had gearbox trouble, necessitating a rush up to Coventry. Salvadori's Maserati was having its brakes relined, and Parnell's tank was completely removed before the car was taken away and sheeted up for the night in a barn…

* * *

Alberto was full of admiration. The way Gigi was handling the Lancia on the wrong side of the road at undiminished speed was masterly. They weren't going to make second practice, of course, but Gigi remained undismayed. Their Maseratis would be waiting for them in perfect order. Guarino Bertocchi could always be trusted. And the friendly Earl Howe would ensure they raced. He was a *grande sportivo*. A *perfetto gentiluomo*.

* * *

Guy Griffiths, wearing his customary safari jacket and beret, headed for the paddocks, a Weston exposure meter round his neck, spare loaded cameras and rolls of film crammed into his jacket pockets. He mainly relied on a 35mm Contax II, a pre-war German camera for which he had several different lenses. Film was still not plentiful after the war, and very often Guy would cut up cine film and load it into cassettes before a meeting.

It was early afternoon. The 500s had come out for their second practice, but there would be plenty of time for Guy to photograph them on race day and too many interesting discussions going on in the Grand Prix paddock to start working. There were rumours that the Ambrosiana Maseratis were on their way to the circuit under RAC escort; that Villoresi and a lesser known Italian, Ascari, were coming too; and that the stewards were having urgent discussions about them. Lord Howe, beaming broadly, was much in evidence.

Guy soon fell in with Peter Whitehead and George Abecassis (who had decided not to race his troublesome new Alta). All the talk was about Howe's insistence on the inclusion of the two Italians. Meanwhile, discussion about the morning's lap times grew and grew. When were they going to be published? Had Chiron's Lago-Talbot really beaten Leslie Johnson's great lap on Thursday?

The Ashmore-Murray Maserati in the pits during first practice day. (*Ferret Fotographics*)

CHAPTER 7

Perhaps the timekeepers were anguishing over inconsistencies in the evidence of their stopwatches; perhaps the circuit's duplicating machine had suffered another unfortunate relapse; or perhaps there had been a breakdown of communication between the timekeepers' hut, the duplicating tent and the Race News Service's former cowshed. Whatever the cause, the delay of the second day's practice times added splendidly to the mounting tension surrounding Saturday's grid. Eventually, before the 500s had finished, the waiting ended. It was true. The old fox was on pole. But there would be some British Racing Green on the front row. Bob Gerard and Leslie Johnson had both made it!

Soon everyone in the paddock was poring over the official list:

Front row:
L. Chiron (2 56.0); E. L. L. de Graffenried (2 57.0); P. Étancelin (2 58.0); F. R. Gerard (2 58.2); L. G. Johnson (2 58.6)

Second row:
B. Bira (2 58.6); R.H. Parnell (2 59.8); P. D. C. Walker (2 59.8); A. P. R. Rolt (3 00.2)

Third row:
T. C. Harrison (3 00.4); G. A. M. Comotti (3 01.0); L. Rosier (3 02.6); J. M. Bolster (3 03.4); G. Richardson (3 03.6)

Fourth row:
G. E. Ansell (3 04.0); G. M. Watson (3 07.0); T. R. Mays (3 07.2); J. D. Hamilton (3 08.0)

Fifth row:
D. A. Hampshire (3 08.2); G. R. Nixon (3 09.4); R. E. Ansell (3 11.0); R. F. Salvadori (3 13.6); S. J. Gilbey (3 20.0)

Louis Chiron's pole position was a vindication for the calculating way in which, in 1947, he had joined Paul Vallée's team. In his distinguished pre-war career, which included twenty Grand Prix wins, Chiron had always found others to fund his racing, but after the war, in his late forties, works drives initially eluded him. So his thoughts turned to Vallée's newly-founded Ecurie France. The more he observed its high standards, the more he inclined towards it.

Vallée was a businessman, just turned forty, who'd made money in haulage, found a rich wife, and, after the war, bought a motorcycle factory and established in the Paris suburb of Aubervilliers his own racing works. He had at once contacted Antonio 'Tony' Lago to get himself into what he was assured would be a privileged relationship with the Talbot Company. In the meantime, he spared no expense in acquiring and developing pre-war Delahayes and Talbots, whose successes on the track with a wide variety of French drivers helped advertise his own off-track business interests.

Chiron, whose incorrigible behind-the-scenes manoeuvres had upset many drivers over the years, decided to pounce. First, he introduced Vallée to a number of good contacts, including Lord Selsdon, who was soon generously loaning his Talbot 26SS (a 1938 model, but expensively converted to Grand Prix specification). Next, Chiron started turning up unexpectedly in the Ecurie's pits, nobly helping out with a stopwatch and any amount of good advice. Above all, his worldly know-how completely dazzled Vallée. Chiron, with his smart Monaco background, was everything Vallée was trying to be: at ease in high society, the perfect party host, someone whose natural ebullience would draw everyone's attention. Accordingly, mid-season, the Ecurie France made a surprise announcement: Chiron would replace the Ecurie's leading driver. Chiron had successfully found a new backer, rich and clever

John Bolster, on the main runway, approaches the Segrave left-hander in Remus, the ex-Bira ERA (R5B). The old RAF hangar in the distance stands between Copse and Maggot's. (*Ferret Fotographics*)

and gullible! And soon the other drivers in the team had to stand aside as he was given his choice of the Ecurie's cars (which, more often than not, fell on the estimable Talbot *Monoplace Centrale* of 1939). He was, of course, still outclassed by the latest Grand Prix machinery, but some solid results in 1948 included second place at Monaco.

As the season unfolded, however, so, too, did Vallée's tale of woe with Lago. Where was the brand new Talbot 26C that Chiron was expecting and Lago had promised? Alas, though Vallée and Chiron were adept in wheeling and dealing, Lago was the supreme master and, realising that his private customers could be squeezed for more cash than Vallée, he kept assuring Vallée that he was, of course, top of the queue, while quietly supplying Rosier, Comotti and others with the first of the 26Cs that came out of his Suresnes factory. But then at last, in late September, there was an end to frustration! The new car had finally materialised. Not only that, it had all the latest factory improvements, making it the fastest new Talbot, as Chiron, smiling with satisfaction, had just proved with pole position.

Though Chiron was understandably pleased to be 2 whole seconds faster than his old rival 'Phi-Phi' Étancelin in the best of the rest of the Lago-Talbots, Étancelin himself was delighted to

Bira approaches Chapel in his Maserati during the second practice day. (*Ferret Fotographics*)

Mechanics with Comotti and Rosier's Talbots, second practice. (*Ferret Fotographics*)

be third fastest and in the centre of the front row. Like Chiron, he had been a big name in the pre-war era, a victor at Le Mans and many Grands Prix. But it had been a struggle to get his businesses back to normal after the long Nazi occupation, and there had been fierce fighting in his part of Normandy after the Allied landings. For the first two years of peacetime, therefore, he had merely kept his hand in with occasional forays in uncompetitive pre-war cars. Two months ago, however, much to Vallée's outrage, he had appeared at Reims with a 26C. This was only his fourth race with it. At fifty-three, the oldest driver in the race, Étancelin was determined that the Lago-Talbot would give his distinguished career a memorable Indian Summer.

He was a good, tough racer, only lacking, perhaps, in that final, special something. He was easily recognisable for his distinctive style – he would saw away at the wheel, even on the straights – and the blue tweed cap that he always wore back to front. Unlike Chiron, he had little knowledge of mechanics, which was probably why he was hard on his machinery, particularly the gearboxes. An effusive character, much more spontaneously so than Chiron, at the smallest declaration of fortune's favour he would plant kisses on the cheeks of all and sundry. Everyone smiled with delight to see him on the front row.

Right: Sam Gilbey's Maserati in the pits with John Wyer (behind the steering wheel), who was involved in its preparation at Monaco's of Watford. (*Ferret Fotographics*)

Opposite: Bira and his Maserati (showing White Mouse logo). (*Ferret Fotographics*)

Another popular character, Toulo de Graffenried, would start between Chiron and Étancelin, having been second quickest in his 4CL. This highly successful Maserati had been much developed since it first appeared in 1939, and de Graffenried's well-developed version was fast enough to beat Parnell and Bira in the latest models. A quick, flamboyant driver now in his mid-thirties, de Graffenried was very much at ease in a team run by Enrico Platé, his fellow Swiss. Platé, who still raced occasionally at the highest level, was an experienced team manager – Tazio Nuvolari had won his final Grand Prix driving for Platé – and was paid well by de Graffenried for taking all the wearisome off-track arrangements out of his hands. Platé would have a well-prepared car waiting for him at each circuit; de Graffenried could concentrate on the driving and the good life.

Fourth fastest was the quiet Bob Gerard, scholarly looking in his spectacles but, at thirty-four, in his prime as a driver. His elegant wife, who herself enjoyed success in hill-climbs, would always put a comb through his hair and try to smarten him up before the victory ceremonies that had been proliferating. *The Autocar* placed him third after Mays and Parnell. He was a quick driver, but he backed up his natural talent with outstanding mechanical preparation. The car that had taken him to the front row of the grid was a ten-year-old ERA (R14B), the second of two he had acquired from Reg Parnell.

The acquisition of the first (R4A) was an instructive occasion. At the end of the war, during which Gerard had worked hard in his family's garage business (Parr's in Leicester), his father offered to buy him a racing car so they drove up to Derby to see Reg Parnell. R4A was in an old shed with six others, all equally woe-begone. The ERA's dashboard had no instruments.

Nuts and screws fell out as the bonnet was opened. Inside they found a collection of plugs, two spanners, the remains of a bird's nest and a decaying glove. Examination of the engine revealed terrible joints with oil leaking everywhere. At £1,000 it was not exactly a snip, but Mr Gerard bought it and, back at the garage, a thorough programme of restoration began.

Leslie Johnson's E-type ERA (GP2, a car built in 1939 whose development had been stopped by the war) was potentially much quicker than Gerard's older B-type, but since acquiring the ERA company the previous November, Johnson had suffered a series of mechanical problems, and he had only made two appearances with it before Silverstone. So his front row position, after just one day's practice, was a real encouragement. The thirty-six-year-old Johnson, who had recently won the Spa 24-hour race in an Aston Martin, had 'often been tipped for stardom' according to *The Autocar*, who ranked him seventh, and Louis Chiron had once declared that he had the flair of Nuvolari. However, his considerable skills were undermined by ill-health and heavy commitments outside motor racing. He ignored as best he could his serious heart and kidney problems, which stemmed from childhood and caused him much discomfort, but he could not ignore his business commitments. He was a self-made man, whose rags-to-riches saga began with an impoverished upbringing in London's East End. While still in his teens, he had transformed his father's struggling cabinet-making business and one successful venture then followed another, his fortune being made in his timber and nuclear energy businesses.

Unaffected by his great wealth, he remained kind and unassuming, an employer who took a genuine interest in the welfare of all his workers. He rarely complained and always

Another photograph of mechanics with Comotti and Rosier's Talbots, second practice. (*Ferret Fotographics*)

thought the best of everyone. Reg Parnell had been horrified to discover a dangerous amount of play in the steering of Johnson's E-type ERA at the Isle of Man. 'You can't race in that, Leslie!' he protested. 'Oh but I must,' replied Johnson. 'They've spent so long in its preparation.' He was the staunchest of friends. Leslie Brooke had come to him with the ambitious idea of an F-type ERA, powered by a V8 engine (funded, like the BRM, by the motor trade) that Brooke himself would build in his metal sheet works at Coventry. Johnson's business instincts doubted the project's validity, but he couldn't let down a friend. The chassis had just been completed…

* * *

The second row consisted of Bira and Parnell's new Maseratis, both of which had disappointed, and the older cars of Walker and Rolt that had done really well. Bira had steadily lowered his lap times but was unhappy not to have been quicker through problems with brakes and steering. Parnell was similarly displeased with his latest 4CLT, a whole second slower than Bira and nearly three behind de Graffenried. He and Wilkie Wilkinson were locked in long discussions, for this was a race he badly wanted to win.

Things could hardly have gone better, however, for thirty-five-year-old Peter Walker and twenty-nine-year-old Tony Rolt. Walker was driving a venerable ERA with which Peter Whitehead had won the Australian Grand Prix before the war. It was a car Walker knew well and only a few weeks before, in pouring rain that soaked his sports jacket, he had made 'one of the most sensational ascents ever seen at Prescott', nearly 3 seconds faster than the champion Mays. The charming Walker was an archetypal racing driver, tall, dark and handsome, and very popular with

the ladies. Son of a Bradford textile merchant and educated at Lancing College, he was known for exciting four-wheel drifts that had earned him the nickname 'Skid Walker'.

Tony Rolt, shortly to retire from the Army, was driving an Alfa Romeo he had bought a year before, one of the 'Bimotore' Alfas built in 1935 with two eight-cylinder engines, one in the front, the

Above: Chiron confers in the pits with Valleé (*top right*) behind his Lago-Talbot.

Opposite: Bill Boddy (*in spectacles, left*) and Louis Rosier (*in overalls, right*) with Rosier's Talbot at the end of the Grand Prix pits, second practice. (*Ferret Fotographics*)

other in the back – a desperate and unsuccessful Italian riposte to the all-conquering Mercedes and Auto Union teams. Rolt's car, sold off by the works and imported into Britain, enlivened Brooklands for a while, but the next owner sensibly had the back engine removed and the rear remodelled, so it was a 'Bimotore' in name only when Rolt subsequently acquired it and enlisted the experienced Freddie Dixon to enlarge its remaining engine to 3.4 litres. It was still something of a monster for someone as inexperienced as Rolt, for whom the Grand Prix would only be the tenth race of his whole career. But he had recently come second in the race that opened the new Zandvoort circuit, and, like the more experienced Walker, was clearly a big talent, fifth in *The Autocar*'s list (which for some strange reason omitted Walker altogether). 'Given the right car,' wrote Sammy Davis perceptively, 'Tony Rolt could become a great name.'

* * *

By contrast, neither Louis Rosier nor Franco Comotti would have been pleased to be so far back as the third row, the performances of their Lago-Talbots looking all the more disappointing in that the three British drivers alongside them, Harrison, Bolster and Richardson, were all in pre-war machinery. Forty-two-year-old Cuth Harrison, who ran a flourishing garage and car dealership in Sheffield, was tenth fastest in Earl Howe's old ERA. A relaxed and fearless driver, Harrison had also driven abroad on occasion on circuits like Spa and Monaco. He nearly won the Ulster Trophy at Ballyclare, only to overturn on the last lap. Not long after his hospitalisation, he was hill-climbing at Prescott and setting the fastest time of the day.

Thirty-seven-year-old John Bolster was similarly fearless. Remus, one of the ERAs from Bira's pre-war stable, had been acquired in 1947 by a rich friend, Peter Bell, for Bolster to drive and himself to manage. With a converted Army lorry for transport and the help of an ex-ERA works mechanic, they had fared well so far. Bolster was passionate about motor sport. He and his brother, when still at Tonbridge School, had built a tiny special, which Bolster developed through the 1930s into one of the most competitive of all specials, 'Bloody Mary'. Costing just £25 originally, it always suffered from unpredictable handling. 'It's not the corners that are difficult,' he once remarked, 'it's those very tricky straight bits in between.'

Bolster had had a distressing war, and rarely mentioned it. He and his brother had long debated over who would run the family farm near Edenbridge and who would fight. Bolster ended up farming; his brother became a pilot and was killed. Further tragedy struck when his first wife died in a road accident with John at the wheel. His extrovert behaviour masked shyness and inner disquiet, but the mask never slipped.

The surprise on the third row was Geoff Richardson, the youngest driver in the race at twenty-four. He had purchased a twelve-year-old special with a Riley engine for £2,000 earlier that year, subsequently working on it in the tuning business he had started in the grounds of his father's farm in Worcestershire, having studied engineering after leaving Rugby School. His competition experience was minimal but he had won, in an old Bugatti, an illegal race in 1947 organised at Silverstone by a local Frazer Nash enthusiast, the so-called 'Mutton Grand Prix' (because of a mishap to an unfortunate sheep). Geoff was so little-known that he was called Guy in Bill Boddy's programme notes, but he was lucky to be racing under any name. Four years earlier, near the end of wartime officer training with the

Royal Armoured Corps at Bovington, he was shot through both legs when a soldier behind him dropped a Sten gun. After spending two years in and out of hospital, he had been left with a pronounced limp.

* * *

The fourth row was all-British. Raymond Mays was disappointed to be 8 seconds slower than Gerard's ERA and alongside the inexperienced trio of Geoff Ansell, Gordon Watson and Duncan Hamilton, all three almost half his age. Geoff Ansell, who farmed 650 acres from a seventeenth-century manor house near Romsey, had purchased his 1936 ERA (R9B) from his cousin Bob a year ago. A former Army captain, he was a promising newcomer who had won at the Isle of Man that year when Parnell's 4CL Maserati had run out of fuel. 'With more experience', commented *The Autocar*, placing him eleventh, 'he may well repeat such success.'

Gordon Watson had started driving young. His father, a director of the family's Dundee-based whisky distillery company, had bought him a Clyno for his twelfth birthday, which Gordon was soon driving with aplomb around the grounds of their estate in the Scottish borders. After his father's death, Gordon came south with his mother to a country house outside Farnham, not too far from Brooklands, where, at the age of eighteen, he first raced a Riley. He had gone to the meeting with his mother and then slipped away quietly, to participate without her knowledge, a ruse that went badly wrong when he overturned directly in front of her. War interrupted Gordon's great passion for fast cars, but after five years with the Royal Artillery he teamed up with an ex-fighter pilot, Robert Cowell, who in 1946 encouraged the purchase of a famous ERA called

Humphrey that had once been raced by Humphrey Cook (ERA's funder and co-founder). Cowell also sold Gordon a 1939 Alta single-seater and persuaded him to buy on their joint behalf an engineering factory in Egham (Leacroft), where the Alta was given the post-war bodywork it had at Silverstone. Not only did Leacroft provide a good base for the pair's racing, but it briefly realised Cowell's dreams of becoming a car constructor. However, his plans for a Cowell-Watson Grand Prix car (funded presumably by Watson) were blown apart, like the partnership, when, in 1948, Cowell embarked on a dramatic change of sex, which, some cynics thought, may have seemed a quicker route to fame and fortune. Gordon Watson, meanwhile, pressed on with his own team at Leacroft that would service several seasons of racing Altas for fun at home and abroad.

The burly Duncan Hamilton, at this time far less experienced than Gordon Watson, shared his desire for fun. He had been educated at Brighton College, flown in the war as a Fleet Air Arm pilot, and had just established his own business in Bagshot, selling second-hand Rolls Royces and Bentleys. He had done really well to make the fourth row with the old 6CM Maserati he had bought earlier in the year from George Abecassis, who had just discovered it lurking in the workshops of the Cape Town Railway Department. (As a new car, it had been sent out to South Africa in 1937 for Villoresi to race.) With a top speed of 140 mph, the 6CM had been highly desirable before its eclipse by the 4CL. But Silverstone would just be Hamilton's fourth race...

* * *

There were five British drivers occupying the fifth and final row. Thirty-year-old Cambridge University graduate David Hampshire lived in some style with his wife in a village outside

Derby and worked for his family's long-established chemical and pharmaceutical business, based in a large, purpose-built factory on the town's outskirts. F. W. Hampshire & Co.'s many medicines included the best-selling cough sweets Zubes ('good for your tubes'). A good friend of Reg Parnell, Hampshire would have expected to be higher up the grid, as his experience went back to pre-war drives at Brooklands and Crystal Palace. He had also raced outside Britain in ERAs, an old Delage and Parnell's own creation, The Challenger. The ERA (R1A) that Hampshire had acquired from Parnell was the very first ERA ever built, proudly unveiled at Brooklands back in May 1934 by Raymond Mays and Humphrey Cook, who both raced it that year. Subsequent owners had included Dick Seaman. Though it was one of the three oldest cars in the race (along with Geoff Richardson's special and Salvadori's Maserati), it had been much modified and in 1948 Hampshire had enjoyed some successes in it.

The inexperienced George Nixon had done well to qualify his recent purchase from Reg Parnell, the second ERA ever built, next to David Hampshire. Humphrey Cook had once driven this car (R2A) to victory on its first race at Brooklands, and Raymond Mays had used it regularly in 1935. Now it belonged to a thirty-five-year-old from Stoke on-Trent, who had only started racing that year but had sensationally won his very first race (the Manx Cup) with a previous purchase, the Leslie Brooke Special. Short and lithe, balding and usually wearing spectacles for his astigmatism, the beautifully spoken Nixon, with his neat moustache, only needed a bowler hat to be the perfect city gentleman. Like Leslie Johnson and Reg Parnell, however, he had come up the hard way.

George's father had been a docker on Tyneside, where he himself was born. His mother encouraged his ambitions, sitting him by the radio to learn to speak like the announcers, and he left grammar school determined to take on the world. In his early twenties he had a pedlar's licence, selling from door to door his own hair tonics, concocted from the ingredients of his more established competitors. He dabbled in scrap metal, promoted and taught ballroom dancing and also joined the Army, rising through the ranks to officer status before being invalided out with serious gastric problems. He was unable to serve in the war, having lost three-quarters of his stomach, but worked hard in the motor trade and by 1948 was the owner of two flourishing Staffordshire garages. Participation in the Silverstone Grand Prix in his first season of racing at the age of thirty-five was a fitting culmination of George's pugnacious approach to life.

Robert 'Bob' Ansell, Geoffrey Ansell's cousin, was disappointed to be on the last row with his 1939 Maserati 4CL. Though this was an older version of de Graffenried's similar model, it was younger than several cars ahead of him. Tenth in *The Autocar*'s ratings, Bob Ansell raced as a hobby, but his experience was greater than that of his younger cousin, extending to foreign tracks like Bremgarten and the Bois de Boulogne and going back to Brooklands. The Ansells' cars were usually garaged at Geoff's Hampshire home, where a friend, George Bainbridge, prepared them. Their reliability record unfortunately seldom matched their smart blue paintwork and red upholstery.

Educated at Malvern, Bob had had been brought up in a manor house outside Stratford-on-Avon, where, in the late 1930s, a gleaming ERA had arrived on his twenty-first birthday.

After distinguished Army service, he had worked his way up in the family's prosperous business (Ansell's, the Birmingham brewers) with all the speed that would be expected of the chairman's nephew. Ever cheerful, he was devoted to country sports and his box at Cheltenham racecourse.

Roy Salvadori's Maserati, which had been raced to victory by 'Nino' Farina in Brno back in its heyday, 1934, was never going to be high up the grid. Son of an Italian immigrant whose ice-cream business was just one of many speculative ventures of varying success, the young Roy proved an adept second-hand car salesman, soon buying a garage in east London, supplying cars for weddings and funerals, before moving west to Fitzrovia, where, like Duncan Hamilton, he supplied the rich with top-quality marques. This had allowed him, at twenty-six, to buy what would be the most venerable Maserati on the grid, the 4CM (which even preceded the 6CM). The ambitious Roy had entered just eight previous races, including drives in an Alfa monoposto once driven by Nuvolari in the German GP of 1935. The 4CM had cost Salvadori £1,250, but this included a deal that its previous owner (Charles Mortimer) would prepare the car at a knock-down price at his Byfleet garage and transport it to meetings. 'The Maserati was a good car,' wrote Salvadori later, 'and very enjoyable to drive; it handled very well, it had excellent brakes and it was almost as fast as the later 6-cylinder model. But the engine peaked at fairly low revs and if I exceeded 6,000 rpm then I was quite likely to do some damage to the engine.'

Last on the grid was Samuel John Gilbey, a forty-year-old electronic engineer from Finchley who owned a Tottenham-based company currently pioneering open reel tape recorders. Another driver with Brooklands experience, Sam had bought his 1937 Maserati 6CM the previous year, a car originally built for one of Villoresi's fellow founders of Scuderia Ambrosiana (Franco Cortese). Prepared for Gilbey at one of the best garages in the country (Monaco's at Watford), the old Maserati had been badly damaged last April at Jersey when Sam had misjudged a corner under braking, mounted a kerb, struck a low wall and found his car somersaulting: 'Gilbey fell out of his Maserati at Marquand's hairpin,' reported *Motor Sport*, 'he and his crash-hat, which had fallen off, being narrowly missed by Bolster, who was following, the driverless car then running badly amok, writing off one of Klementaski's expensive cameras and nearly Klem himself, and finishing up against a Vauxhall saloon parked in a garage yard – this might have been a really nasty incident'. The ever-thoughtful Lord Howe, one of the race stewards, had rushed to the pits to reassure Sam's wife that he was all right.

* * *

Five cars failed to make the grid (which had been limited to twenty-five). Lord Selsdon and Lord Waleran had entertained few hopes of qualification in their elderly Talbot; their presence all along had been as a helpful backup for Ecurie France. It was likewise never in sight for Bobbie Baird, the son of a Belfast newspaper proprietor, who had bought Paul Emery's latest Special and installed a big but elderly Duesenberg motor in it. Despite the attentions of Emery, a talented engineer, the Emeryson kept boiling and catching fire. Alastair Archie 'Buster' Baring, however, had ambitions to make the cut. A Berkshire-based timber and builder's merchant who had hill-climbed a Bugatti before the war, he perhaps hoped for more out of his Maserati 6CM than it could provide.

Fred Ashmore, who was sharing his Maserati 4CL with David Murray, its prospective purchaser, would probably have qualified

The RAF Guardhouse at the old entrance, seen here in the 1960s, was one of Silverstone's most important buildings in the time of Villoresi and Ascari. (*BRDC Archive*)

it, had not Murray (a thirty-eight-year-old Scottish accountant and entrepreneur who had recently come into money) crashed the Maserati heavily into marker drums in second practice, seriously damaging the steering. Ashmore, who had raced on the continent with Reg Parnell in impressive places like Nîmes, Nice, Reims and Comminges, was another wonderfully vivid character. As a young boy he had run away to a travelling circus and his ability to get into scrapes and squabbles like *Carousel*'s Billy Bigelow had characterised his subsequent career in the garage trade. Fred was not best pleased with David Murray for ruining their race prospects, but at least he persuaded him to buy the now outdated car.

Leslie Brooke, the final non-starter, had recorded a time on Thursday (in an ERA, R7B, bought from Parnell) that would have put him close to the third row, but unfortunately damage in second practice put him out of the race. The frustration of learning that his new Maserati was held up in the Italian customs could well have added force to the lurid slides in his cornering, but the bravery that had won him the George Medal during the Coventry blitz (for spending three hours in a burning building as he freed people trapped in a cellar) was always there in his driving. *The Autocar*, in ranking him sixth, hinted at his general belligerence: 'Leslie Brooke, who has the determination but not the balance of Seaman, will not let anything stop him getting up in front. In his exuberance he may go too fast, but he may also become our most forcing driver.' A Coventry-based engineer and precious metals dealer, now in his late thirties, Brooke might well have made as big a name for himself as his friend Parnell with just a little more luck.

CHAPTER 8

The 500s were out practising in mid-afternoon when a posse of smart RAC motorcyclists coming up the entrance road heralded the arrival of a weary-looking Lancia Aprilia and an unusually long lorry, a Dodge 3-tonner, built to carry bomber crews around USAF aerodromes but converted to a new role that allowed it to carry the two Ambrosiana Maseratis. After much gesticulation and no little sounding of horns, it was waved onto the circuit where it did a slow lap, much to the interest of passing 500s, before pulling in by the footbridge to the paddock.

One of the first to greet Gigi and Alberto was Giulio Ramponi, who, twenty-five years earlier, had been a young mechanic with Antonio Ascari's Alfa Romeo in the days when mechanics rode as passengers in Grand Prix, a practice which was only stopped in 1925, the year Ascari was killed. Ramponi had left fascist Italy in the early 1930s to set up a business in London (which included servicing Dick Seaman's famous Delage) and was now rebuilding his career, interrupted by wartime internment in the Isle of Wight, as trade representative for Lodge and Vandervell.

As Gigi and Alberto were hurried away to refresh themselves under a nearby tap and change into driving clothes, it was announced that the stewards had agreed the new arrivals could have four timed laps to allow race qualification. The two

Above: Ascari and Villoresi in the paddock late Friday afternoon, just before the extra practice session. (*Guy Griffiths Collection*)

Opposite: Villoresi chats in the heart of the paddock, near the farm. The building on the right (no longer standing) hides the farmhouse. (*Guy Griffiths Collection*)

Maseratis were swiftly towed to the Shell Mex fuelling bay (a couple of petrol pumps installed alongside the brick wall of one of the farm's outhouses) and thence across the grass to the scrutineers' tent, where Henry Godfrey gave them a cursory check. Godfrey was a distinguished motoring designer and engineer, the 'G' of his surname commemorated forever in the GN and HRG marques that he had helped create. He'd already seen the supposedly similar models of Parnell and Bira, and it didn't take long to notice that the Italians' 4CLT/48s had different superchargers and brakes.

The 500s had completed their practice session by the time Gigi and Alberto appeared in the pits, where many other teams were still working. The extra practice session was held in an atmosphere of party-like informality. The rain clouds of the early afternoon were taking their leave. There were no marshals on the circuit. And opposite the pits, where last-minute work was going on with the roofing of the grandstand, a van and motorcycle stood parked beside the track. The indefatigable Bill Boddy was there to record it all:

> Ascari and the smiling Villoresi arrive, the latter intrigued by a passing Meteor jet fighter. Ramponi gives advice, Mrs Petre promises Villoresi a cherry-brandy that evening to compensate for a fearful journey, and everywhere is excitement and suspense. Bira and his crew still labour in his Maserati, Holgate telling Villoresi amid much mirth, that bits of the steering are made of cheese. Villoresi has car 4CLT-1594, Ascari 4CLT-1597, identified, at least until they warm up, by white and blue blanking strips in their radiator grills.

Above: Part of the modern farm. The Grand Prix paddock was largely situated behind and to the right of the red-tiled building. The entrance to the track (which ran along the back of the white-roofed farm building) was just 80 yards away, down the narrow road to the left.

Opposite: Another modern view, looking at the area where Villoresi was standing (*as seen on page 67, but from the opposite direction*)

Inset: Villoresi brings his Maserati out of the paddock for his qualification laps, late on Friday afternoon, passing Col. Barnes' parked Healey. (*Ferret Fotographics*)

Villoresi has his 'Jersey' mechanic, both drivers a sort of personal manager in attendance. With but a short push the engines start and run with a harsh, clean note. Bira shows Villoresi the race distance and laps, bonnets are replaced and locked with fasteners, even these have lightening holes, and out they go. After a brief stop for new plugs they really get down to it, in company with Bira, Richardson's ERA-Riley and Chiron's Talbot.

* * *

These few laps of extra practice were a good opportunity for Guy Griffiths to prepare for the next day's races. He had taken a few photographs by the pits and paddock, concentrating on the new arrivals, but he hadn't enough film to be prodigal. He made his way over the footbridge and experimented with shots of the cars approaching the start-line. Dissatisfied with the flat background, he walked on past the grandstand and hangar to the exit of Abbey. It was hardly as photogenic as Jersey or the Isle of Man, but the cars looked better there, under cornering stress.

It was over in twenty minutes. Ascari (2 54.6) was quicker than Villoresi (2 56.4) though the validity of these timings was a little suspect, almost half the motoring press declaring that Villoresi was the faster. It had been agreed that the Italians' Maseratis would start from the back of the grid, but the lap times suggested they were still favourites for the race.

Not to have allowed the colourful Italians to participate would have severely damaged the Grand Prix even to the point of credibility. Nonetheless, it was later remarked in certain disgruntled quarters that the stewards did seem to be operating two sets of rules, for the 500 driver Laurie Bond (who would find future fame via his Bond three-wheelers) was similarly late arriving but had not been given an extra practice session.

* * *

The final times for the 500s had been swiftly published. Yet again there was one pre-eminent driver: Stirling Moss. On the Thursday, Moss' cream Cooper had been 10 seconds faster than its nearest rival. On the Friday it would have stretched the gap to 12 seconds, but for Spike Rhiando, a new arrival, who had managed to take 3 seconds out of the 12.

Spike Rhiando was the biggest personality in the 500 paddock, someone who set out to be noticed by wearing ultra-colourful clothes, often as outrageously Texan as the Buick saloon that towed his new Cooper (anodised in bright gold and quickly nicknamed 'the banana split'). Alvin James Spike Rhiando was the self-titled 'American dirt track ace', a former speedway star who'd been king of midget racing and, before that, a great circus performer. He'd written most entertaining articles about his exciting past in the popular press: 'Round the Wall of Death on Roller Skates', 'Thrown out of my Car into the Crowd', 'Adventures with the Stars in Hollywood' and 'Dodging Snipers on a Motor Bike'. Spike Rhiando was American as blueberry pie – or so, at least, ran the gossip around Silverstone that afternoon.

The truth was a little different. His real name was Albert Stevens and he had been brought up in London, son of an English juggler and German circus performer, but, as an obscure speedway rider

Opposite: Villoresi and de Graffenried in discussion behind Bira's Maserati just before the extra practice session, Friday. (*Ferret Fotographics*)

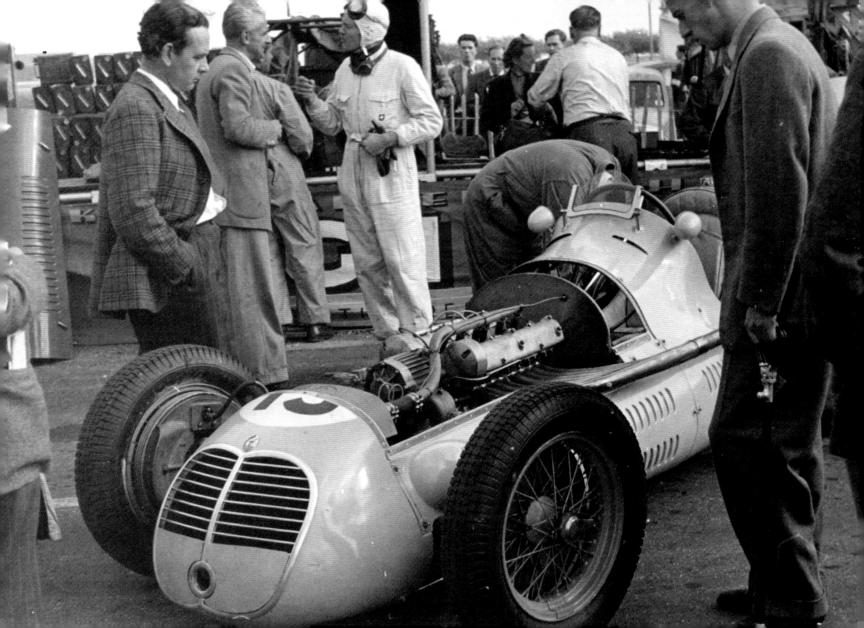

Above: Bira takes his Maserati out on to the track for extra practice, Friday evening. (*Ferret Fotographics*)

Opposite: Bira (with Stanley Holgate in overalls) in the pits, Friday evening. The lower part of the old airfield's water tower is visible in the background and part of the only hangar that still survives. (*Guy Griffiths Collection*)

in the 1930s, he had campaigned (in East Anglia) as Alvin James Franchetti and (at Dagenham, where he was a useful reserve) as Spike Antonio Riando. After some unexceptional midget racing in America he had briefly introduced the sport to west London. During the war, he had worked for the English branch of the American Caterpillar tractor firm. Afterwards, he put his considerable knowledge of earth-shifting to excellent use, homing in on the Attlee government's disastrous ground nut scheme in Tanganyika, the considerable profits from which had enabled Spike to purchase an estate in Surrey and to be racing a newly acquired Cooper 500 with a lavish budget. And now, at thirty-eight, reborn as a wide-grinning Texan, he was certainly showing that he knew how to throw a 500 around rather better than most.

Third on the 500 grid – and a distinct contrast to Rhiando – was a modest forty-year-old Harrow garage owner, Colin Strang, in his own Strang special. One of the 500 pioneers, whose original Fiat-based 500 had been much copied, he seldom talked about his past exploits, though these had included rowing many miles across open seas in a small boat to avoid capture by the Japanese.

The lap times clearly showed that Strang, Rhiando and all those other hopefuls on the grid next day would have a struggle coping with Stirling Moss, whose Cooper was clearly being driven with that extra something that only the specially-gifted possess. The quality of preparation on Moss' car was also exceptional, a harbinger, indeed, of a new professionalism that was to come into the sport. Austen May, who bought Moss' Cooper at the end of the 1948 season, was amazed at the scrupulous care that had been invested in its every detail by the Moss entourage:

Throughout the vehicle ordinary locknuts had everywhere been replaced by the Simmonds self-locking nuts; extensive wiring and split-pinning had been resorted to, to offset that number one bogey of a single-cylinder engine, vibration; much of the chassis and body framework had been drilled for lightness; the rear shock absorbers had been remounted; small cooling ducts had been added to the front brakes. The Speedway JAP engine had been converted from a 5-stud to 4-stud, which simply means that only four cylinder-head holding-down bolts were employed instead of five. The internals were polished literally to a mirror finish … A light-sprung steering wheel padded at the centre against possible crash injury replaced the original wheel…

* * *

It was party time. Bill Boddy departed rather later than most, for he had so much he had wanted to check. When at last he reached the Dadford Road in his 'faithful and economical Vauxhall Ten', the traffic had mostly cleared and he could floor the accelerator. Sweeping up the October leaves as he headed south on a country road at over 50 mph was exhilarating. The auspices seemed good for race day.

CHAPTER 9

Bill Boddy was back by the time the gates opened at 8.00 a.m. on race day, an excited passenger in the rear seat of a type 44 Bugatti of late 1920s vintage. But if this encouraged thoughts of Brooklands with the 'right crowd and no crowding', they were misleading, for traffic was already homing in from all parts of the country. A crowd of around 130,000 was on its way.

'CARS, CARS and STILL MORE CARS' ran the *Buckingham Advertiser*'s headline. The town, through which all of the traffic from the south had to pass, had 'awoken on Saturday to find itself the centre of the modern urge of speed'. From 'the first streak of dawn' there had been 'a ceaseless procession of cars of all makes, ages and types…' It was not until well after 11.45 a.m., the time when the opening ceremony was due to start, that it abated. Beyond the town, along Stowe Avenue, there was 'a majestic procession' comparable with 'the noble picture of the funeral of the Comte de Paris', except that it now consisted of cars rather than horses. 'The normally peaceful village of Dadford was agog with excitement and the villagers turned out in full force to watch the procession.'

Brackley's local newspaper compared 'the 4-hour unbroken line of cars' coming in from the west to 'an endless railway train'. On the Northampton road, traffic from the north and east was more like a train stuck at the signals, a queue stretching back past Towcester. And soon there were queues all around the circuit despite the drafting of extra police into the surrounding towns where some stayed on duty for up to thirteen hours.

Spectators also poured in by train and coach. The old steam railway network, just nationalised by the Attlee government, offered considerable choice. Buckingham was the closest station to Silverstone for those coming from the south, but involved a diversion from the former LNWR line from Euston onto a slow branch line. Much better were the expresses from London stopping at Brackley en route to Manchester after only 80 minutes. From the north, the old LMS trains, en route to Euston, stopped at Blisworth. From the north-east it was easier to make for Northampton. At all these stations a large number of pre-war coaches and charabancs had been specially gathered, ready to play their part in the growing traffic congestion.

The RAC had produced a helpful flyer suggesting the best routes for all those arriving for 'an afternoon of thrilling sport – the fastest cars being driven by the fastest drivers in Europe!' It was sensibly cautious about the kind of facilities the spectators would find. 'The Royal Automobile Club, in reintroducing motor racing of Grand Prix standard into this country, craves the indulgence of patrons of the sport'. Accommodation and amenities would not be 'as perfect as the Club would wish since eight months' organisation has had to be achieved within a period of eight weeks'. No specific inadequacies were given – to write about the absence of proper lavatories might have scared thousands away – though there was a veiled hint about the possibility of mud in wet weather: 'Car parking and other public viewpoints are of necessity mainly on grass enclosures. Spectators are advised to bring waterproofs and stout footwear.'

To the race-starved enthusiasts of 1948 it would all have sounded like a terrific adventure: grassy enclosures, a day out in the country, a Grand Prix amid fields of corn, surrounded by nostalgic mementoes of Bomber Command. And the RAC were suggesting that they might well be in at the beginning of something really big: 'It is intended, with the continued valued support of the Public, that conditions for future events to be held on the Circuit will be vastly improved and of a more permanent nature ... The Club regrets that conditions in this inaugural meeting will not be up to the standard it will certainly set itself in the future.'

The RAC, in the business of solving problems on the road, had done all it could in the limited time to ease traffic congestion, but there was only one entrance for the general public and that was on the narrow Dadford lane. Long delays were inevitable and, as such, cheerfully tolerated on the whole. Post-war Britain was conditioned to long queues. Those who queued for a loaf of bread or a string of sausages would expect to queue for a Grand Prix. Collecting entrance money from the majority who had not pre-booked was a necessarily lengthy business, though cars were charged 30s regardless of the number of passengers.

(Motorbikes cost 10s, small coaches £5 and large coaches £7 10s 0d.) A Westminster Bank bullion van plied between the various sales points, collecting cash.

There were four large public enclosures, all outside the old aerodrome's perimeter road, where spectators could park their cars: B, around Woodcote; C, along the straight leading to Copse; D, between Copse and Maggot's; and E, between Becket's and Chapel. Entry to these enclosures was of necessity by the perimeter road.

There were two further, specially privileged enclosures, each with its own narrow means of entrance from the Dadford lane. Enclosure A, for members of the RAC and allied clubs (still costing the regulation 30 shillings per car), occupied the area between the exit from Club Corner to the apex of Abbey Curve. And adjacent to this, all along the straight from Abbey to the entrance road before Woodcote, Enclosure F (the area littered with old RAF buildings including two hangars) had been designated for those with grandstand tickets. The pre-booked grandstand tickets cost £2 and car parking just 10s extra.

The arrangement looked excellent on paper and it probably would have worked with a smaller volume of traffic. The police looking after the Dadford lane did all they could to keep things going, but in the general melee many grandstand ticket holders were diverted into Enclosures A and B, and others without grandstand tickets into the pre-booked enclosure F, where 'no machinery existed for collecting fees'. Others looking for F and A were diverted into the main entrance, after which they had to join a barely moving cavalcade down the track past the pits. The 122 helpers employed by the RAC 'for supervising traffic and parking' stood by helplessly; so too did the sixty police inside.

Amid all the mayhem many thousands entered without paying, some because gate-keepers had run out of change and just let everyone in, others by taking advantage of the situation.

Geoffrey Samuelson wrote afterwards that 'pedestrian control was impossible while it is so easy to penetrate the airfield at numerous places.' Mr Whetstone, of the Road Patrols Dept, noted that the special ticket sales gate provided for Silverstone villagers had been less popular than routes 'through adjacent hedges'. Meanwhile, pedestrians from the Dadford direction sauntered through the woods and entered the circuit unofficially, thereby saving 7s 6d per person.

The earliest arriving spectators, finding nothing much to do but listen to music from the public address speakers, took the opportunity of examining the circuit, swarming all over the track, crowding the pits and trampling over crops as they sought short cuts across the infield. Some shrewder ones carried off straw bales to make their own grandstands. As numbers grew, so the congestion of spectators and their cars along the pits straight grew worse. Jimmy Brown later wrote sharply to Geoffrey Samuelson:

> Approximately 20,000 cars used part of the racing circuit before racing commenced. The track had been prepared and stones were dislodged by spectators' cars. It is possible for oil to be deposited from these cars or litter to be thrown onto the track, some of it being highly dangerous to racing cars. In no other sport are spectators allowed on the track, field, arena etc in cars or on foot.

The Chief Marshal of Crowd Control, tasked with liaising with the car parks and police, was Wing Commander G. F. Turberville, from the RAC's Touring Department, whose wartime expertise was in air traffic control. Turberville soon discovered that the paucity of police numbers was exacerbated by the circuit's position on the Bucks–Northants borders. Superintendent Chapman, of the Northants Constabulary, was making decisions for some of the circuit, while other parts came under the Bucks Constabulary, who preferred to do things their way. Turberville's main ally was Northamptonshire's chief constable, Captain Bolton, who, after much forward planning with Geoffrey Samuelson, had chosen as his headquarters the airfield's Control Tower, a two-storey building with a helpfully flat roof. Bolton had any number of large-scale maps installed there, as well as the very latest wireless and walkie-talkie technology. A stationary wireless van had been strategically placed at Towcester and another in Buckingham. In the aerodrome itself there were no less than five walkie-talkie points so that Captain Bolton, as he prowled around the Control Tower's roof with his binoculars, had everywhere within a radius of 20 miles under his control. That, at least, had been the theory. In the event, Bolton spent most of the morning in helpless radio communication with his aides, receiving one gloomy report after another.

At around 11.30 a.m., shortly before John Cobb was to open the circuit, all entering traffic was stopped coming out on to the track, causing a complete blockage on the main entrance road, until the more adventurous began rally-crossing their way into enclosure A or breaking into the old airfield's heartland, an area only intended for the grandstand ticket holders. Fencing off the grandstands had not been deemed necessary and there was soon chaos around them. A later report, written to Samuelson by Mr R. Alexander of the RAC's Associate Members' Department, gave some details. At 8.30 a.m. he had taken up his position 'on the concrete leading to the Grandstand area' to collect the customers' ticket vouchers and direct them to the correct grandstand. While the grass around the concrete was wet with early morning dew, a steady queue approached him. But grey skies were soon changing to blue – it was going to be a really sunny day – and the grass quickly dried.

> There was no way of stopping people getting past me. The job itself was more than one person could handle. I was assailed by the flood of people who insisted that they had some official connection with the race, but who could not produce any documentary evidence to support their claim. Such people were politely but very firmly shooed away, except in one or two instances when they pushed their way past and I was unable to take any steps to stop them. A number of individuals who claimed connection with the canteens (i.e. drivers of motor vehicles and their helpers) floated about the area but few of them appeared to have any means of identification.

Things got progressively worse:

> I was further assailed by many people clamouring to get to the track … Several motor vehicles attempted to make use of the approach giving a variety of reasons, some drivers stating that they had competitors' cars, some stating that they had been directed to that point as they were conveying invalids who couldn't walk, and some claiming to be connected to the caterers. None of these vehicles had any distinctive marking to enable me to deal with them.

Many people, acting as officials, 'attempted to introduce personal friends, who were not themselves in possession of a ticket or any form of pass'.

Alexander clearly did not want his superiors to think him inefficient, and the admission that 'many people gained access to the Grandstand area in a manner over which I had no control whatever' was softened by as many positives as he could muster. 'Generally speaking everybody was good-humoured and took any instructions I gave in good heart (with the exception of one or two obstreperous people).' The catering marquee behind the grandstands had been splendidly busy. And he himself had been able to address a pressing need: 'You will appreciate that lavatories were in great demand by the huge crowd. Some people seemed to have considerable difficulty in finding them. On a number of occasions I had to allow access to the Grandstand area to people requiring the use of these conveniences.' The old RAF latrines nearby were probably a rather more attractive option than Jimmy Brown's alternatives.

Alexander, whose trying vigil finally ended at 3.00 p.m., gently concluded that perhaps in the future the grandstands should have more than one overseer.

Opposite: Great interest around the 500s pits the morning before the race. (*Guy Griffiths Collection*)

CHAPTER 10

The official opening of the circuit by John Cobb at 11.45 a.m. marked the start of the day's commentaries on the public address system by two journalists, *The Motor*'s Rodney Walkerley (from the start line) and *The Autocar*'s John Dugdale (from the Segrave-Seaman intersection). Walkerley's tall figure had long been a familiar one at races both home and abroad. A flamboyant individual, now in middle age, with an infectious enthusiasm for all motor sport, he had just been elected both to the BRDC (usually only open to racing drivers) and the RAC's Competition Committee. He had also been an active member of Howe's Grand Prix sub-committee. Sitting cramped inside his little box by the start-line, a supply of cigarettes and whisky on the table in front of him, he now began the introductions to the opening ceremony in his usual relaxed and avuncular style, addressing his listeners courteously as 'ladies and gentlemen', for that had always been the way at Brooklands.

John Cobb, explained Walkerley, was, as everyone knew, the current holder of the world's land speed record, which he had raised last year in his two runs over a measured mile at the Bonneville Salt Flats to 394.197 mph, in the course of which he had become the first man on earth ever to travel at over 400 mph. Educated at Eton and Cambridge, Cobb was now forty-eight years old, and when not breaking land speed records, he was working in the City of London in the family's prosperous fur business. He was also famous before the war for racing monster cars and was the holder of the Brooklands outright lap record, achieving over 143 mph in his Napier-Railton in 1935.

The track is about to be opened, ladies and gentlemen, by a man who knows all about speed and old airfields, for Group Captain John Cobb also spent five wartime years in the RAF. Here he is, ladies and gentlemen, opening the Silverstone Circuit in a Healey Sportsmobile.

Cobb eased the convertible, with its hood down, carefully out of the paddock and down the track between the pits and grandstands. Cellulosed in 'jewellescent green', it was somewhat flashier than the sober black Humber in which he had driven up from London. In his smart pin-striped suit and black tie, Cobb looked a little incongruous, though a jaunty country cap added a little levity to the occasion. A charming but deeply reticent individual, he was usually monosyllabic in interviews and currently even more taciturn than ever, for it was only months since the biggest tragedy of his life, the death of his wife, Elizabeth. For years he had decided that his passion for speed and danger debarred him from marriage, and so he had lived with his mother at the family home in Esher, until in 1947, shortly before the latest successful record attempt, he had been persuaded to marry the delightful Elizabeth. And now, after a painful illness and only fourteen months of marriage, she was gone. So it was good to get away from the waving crowds at Copse and head the Sportsmobile into the solitude of a long runway.

Isn't the Healey Sportsmobile fabulous, ladies and gentleman? One of only a handful so far produced by Donald Healey's exciting new company, a big car with really striking lines, its Riley engine taking it to a prodigious 100 mph!

The pleasing solitude continued, for there were only a handful of officials at the remote Segrave Corner. Henry Segrave! Cobb had known him first at Eton. Segrave had been three years his senior and he had followed his subsequent career avidly. Indeed, Segrave had been his inspiration, first at Brooklands and later winning the land speed record in his Golden Arrow. His subsequent successful attack on the water speed record, though it had ended in tragedy, was something that was currently preoccupying him.

Right: One of the TT-winning motorcycles being ridden through the paddock to participate with John Cobb in the circuit's official opening ceremony. (*Guy Griffiths Collection*)

It's a wonderful cavalcade, isn't it, ladies and gentleman? First that triumph of post-war British engineering with the great John Cobb at the wheel, and then his outriders, the three motorcyclists who won for Britain at the TT races at the Isle of Man this year, Freddie Frith, Maurice Cann and Artie Bell. Give them a good wave, too, ladies and gentlemen! Later on, during the Grand Prix, all three will be acting as a high speed patrol for the Clerk of the Course, Colonel Barnes.

Cobb marvelled at the packed crowds between Maggot's and Chapel before luxuriating in the solitude of the Hangar Straight, Stowe Corner and the climb back to the centre of the track at Seaman. Then more packed crowds, from Club to the start-line, where he turned gratefully into the paddock, his duty done. The circuit had been officially opened. Cobb could return to the life he really liked, being a steward at race meetings with the opportunity to chat to like-minded devotees. He must catch up with George (Eyston), his fellow Silverstone steward and land speed record-breaker. He also wanted to catch up with one of the race judges, his good friend Oliver Bertram, from whom he had wrested the outright Brooklands lap record. But first he must try and avoid that fellow with the BBC microphone, looming towards him...

* * *

Guy Griffiths was waiting to photograph the start of Silverstone's very first race from the far side of the track from the pits. Across the road, Howe was already standing on his chair with his Union Jack, but the 500s looked anything but ready.

The race had attracted an entry of thirty-four drivers, twenty-six of whom were to race. Their backgrounds were as varied as their experience and age. Completing the front row with Moss,

Rhiando, Coward and Strang was 'Curly' Dryden, landlord of The Royal George, Dorchester-on-Thames, a former Squadron Leader and fighter pilot, shot down over the North Sea. On the second row: three young men from London – Cooper Cars' John Cooper, Eric Brandon, who ran an electrical wholesale business, and Stan Coldham, a master butcher – alongside an Old Etonian of rising sixty, Sir Francis Samuelson, a Sussex farmer who had been racing since 1908. On row three: Charlie Smith from Battersea, a young motorcyclist just starting his own small engineering business; Wing Commander Frank Aikens, a serving officer with the RAF with a penchant for deerstalkers and the best handlebar moustache in the paddock; George Saunders, a Surbiton restaurant owner and former speedway rider; and Bill Grose, who was supplying Jimmy Brown with breakdown vehicles from his family's Northampton garage.

Lower down the grid, entries included Flight Lieutenant Dickie Stoop, driving a 'Spink 500' in his very first race; Dennis Flather, a wealthy Sheffield steel merchant; Ken Wharton, the current RAC British Trials champion, a thirty-two-year-old motor engineer and Ford dealer from Birmingham, who had started racing in 1935 and had built his own Special for this meeting on an Austin 7 chassis; Joe Fry from Bristol, a member of the Fry chocolate family, one of the leading drivers in his

Opposite: Spike Rhiando (*in cardigan, centre*) going out with his Cooper to the track from the 500s paddock (*to the right of the picture*), wearing the clothes he raced in. RAC patrolmen stand at the ready in the mid-distance. (*Guy Griffiths Collection*)

Freikaiserwagen but down the grid after major mechanical problems; David Macpherson (2nd Baron Strathcarron), son of a minister in Lloyd George's cabinet, educated at Eton and Cambridge and a wartime pilot of Wellingtons, currently, at twenty-four, a second-hand car salesman; Ken Smith, manager of the Jolly Farmers, Enfield; a Kettering taxi proprietor, A. A. D. Underwood; and R. W. Messenger, a building contractor from Banbury.

The start proved an embarrassing shambles. Many of the drivers showed little concern at the display of the 3-minute board or its successors, few engines being started on the 1-minute board. Though Lord Howe was ready to start the race, there were mechanics and hangers-on all over the grid, some drivers were out of their cars, plugs were being changed and petrol tanks topped up. The race was scheduled for 12 noon, but when Howe flagged it away at precisely that time, less than a third of the field was ready.

Moss and Strang, from opposite ends of the front row, made strong starts, but in the centre Dryden and Coward still had their mechanics with them and though Spike Rhiando's helpers had disappeared, his 'Banana Split' had a dead engine. Dryden eventually got going, followed by Coward, but Spike remained motionless, waiting for a push-start. Behind him all four cars on the second row were unready, so there was limited room for others to come through. The space left by Moss, however, was enthusiastically seized by Wing Commander Frank Aikens, who had swerved past the stationary John Cooper in front of him, had passed Coward and Dryden, and was in zealous pursuit of Moss and Strang. Spike Rhiando was eventually tenth away, having been push-started by Stirling Moss' father and young mechanic.

Moss and Strang, meanwhile, realising that some kind of problem had led to their isolation at the head of the field, momentarily slowed down in a gesture of good sportsmanship. And so, as the 500s approached the huge crowd at Woodcote, Moss was holding a tight inside line with Aikens drifting wide alongside and Dryden following Moss closely. Strang, who had been passed by Dryden, had missed the apex, and so too Coward, behind him. The leading five cars were some distance ahead of three Coopers from the second row – Cooper himself, Samuelson and Coldham – and Spike Rhiando, up to ninth. There was then a huge gap. The remaining sixteen cars had yet to clear the grandstands.

About 3 minutes later, they were back, with Moss leading from Strang, Dryden and Cooper, and Rhiando up to eighth. Wing Commander Aikens, gallantly pitting his homebuilt special against all the factory Coopers, was holding on in sixth. Guy Griffiths, meanwhile, had walked down the side of the track to Abbey, where Moss passed by, leading on lap 3, pursued by Strang, Dryden and Rhiando (who had overtaken John Cooper). Finding spectators curiously barred from Club, except at the exit, Guy crossed the track and walked briskly up the runway to the intersection, where Seaman and Segrave offered better photographic opportunities. Rhiando by this time had moved up to a comfortable second place on the retirement of Strang and Dryden with engine problems and, to Guy's surprise, began drawing much closer to Moss. Soon there was a duel developing between Moss and Rhiando, who were both well in front of the rest of the field. It later transpired that Rhiando had installed a specially tuned engine after second practice that had been lent him by Harringay's Australian speedway champion, Vic Duggan.

The Motor

For the Best Reports and Pictures

Strang and Moss (5) lead off at the chaotic start of the 500s race. (*Guy Griffiths Collection*)

On the fifth lap there was drama at the central intersection. Moss was out of his car and sprinting across the fields from Seaman to the pits, having lost all drive from a fractured engine sprocket. Spike was now leading the race by over half a minute. The disappointed Moss was soon running back, tools in hand, but, by the time he effected a repair, the 50-mile race distance was nearly up and Spike Rhiando was on his thirteenth and last lap, still well in the lead despite the smoke now coming from his special engine, suggesting imminent seizure. His fuel tank had also developed a split (the after-effects of a bad crash at a hill-climb the week before) and methanol was leaking onto his shoulders and back. Despite considerable pain, the tough Rhiando made the chequered flag and, after 47 minutes of racing, won the £50 first prize. He had finished 6 seconds ahead of John Cooper (£30) who was himself 30 seconds ahead of Sir Francis Samuelson, the last of the prize-winners (£20) in what had ended up as something of a dour procession. Coopers occupied the first four places, Rob Coward, fifth of the eight finishers, being the first privateer. Rhiando's average time was 60.68 mph, impressive on a course which, for all the long runways, had six very slow corners.

Spike's colourful shirt was the worse for being soaked in methanol and, at his request, Rodney Walkerley appealed over the PA for a spare shirt. Around 100 potential donors of both sexes quickly rushed forward. Legend also has it that an appeal went out for the loan of a pair of trousers, too. If so, that queue was probably even longer.

Reg Phillips approaches Segrave Bend in the strange-looking Fairley 500. (*Guy Griffiths Collection*)

CHAPTER 11

Wilfrid Andrews had a good idea. The Control Tower, with its flat roof and unusual exterior iron staircase, would make the ideal venue for the buffet lunch planned for local dignitaries and other important guests. Samuelson's gentle protestations that it had been allocated already to Captain Bolton were swept aside. There would be no problems in the Control Tower's dual role; the traffic jams would be in the morning before lunch, by which time the good Captain Bolton would surely have put all his maps away. He and his wife should be added to the guest list.

Andrews and Samuelson were at the foot of the Control Tower at 12.45 p.m., ready to host their lunch party in the October sunshine. The line of apple trees that stretched away behind them rustled gracefully under blue skies. There was an all-pervasive smell of fresh-mown grass. Even the crumbling farmhouse, one of whose rooms was currently used for potato storage, contrived to look picturesque.

The party was soon in full swing. As Andrews and Samuelson detached themselves from a discussion with Captain Bolton on the pros and cons of walkie-talkies and gazed out at the animation all around, they could feel justly proud of the eight-week transformation of the old aerodrome. 'The vast assemblage of cars in the parking grounds' was, in the words of a local reporter, 'positively dazzling'. And so vast was the airfield that, however dense the crowds, there was still 'a sense of sublime spaciousness'. In the lunch interval it had suddenly become 'a huge pleasure ground' as thousands unwrapped their spam sandwiches, 'relaxing on the grass and basking in sunshine'. The refreshment buffets were thriving; the ladies of Silverstone, dressed daintily for the occasion, were helping out magnificently. Iced cakes, fresh and stale, were devoured hungrily; ice-cream vendors had rarely smiled so much since the declaration of peace.

The RAC's party at the Control Tower was bringing a brief touch of Pall Mall distinction to the rural south midlands, and society magazines later listed some of the celebrities there: the 9th Duke of Richmond and Gordon, who had raced at Brooklands and was currently developing the Goodwood circuit on his estate; Earl Howe and his wife, chatting to the 5th Marquess Camden; the forty-year-old Viscount Curzon, Howe's son by his first marriage; the Hon. Cyril Siddeley, the future Lord Kenilworth; Sir Algernon Lee Guinness, who had set the land speed record of 121 mph back in 1908, and Captain George Eyston, three times the record holder, whose Thunderbolt had clocked 357 mph; John Cobb, of course, and another of the big pre-war Brooklands favourites,

Jack Dunfee, one of the famous 'Bentley Boys', whose brother Clive had been killed going over the banking.

Among the many local dignitaries were the Hon. John Fermor-Hesketh of Cosgrove Hall, brother of the 2nd Baron Hesketh of Easton Neston; Roger Gresham-Cooke, currently the Director of the Society of Motor Manufacturers and Traders; the Grafton Hunt's Master (Maj. Leslie Huggins) and Secretary (Col. Toler Aylward); Sir Everard Duncombe of Great Brickhill Manor,

the next High Sheriff of Buckinghamshire; and Maj. Reginald Manningham-Buller of Greens Norton, the MP for Daventry.

The guests had much to chatter about. Above all, there was the splendour of the new circuit. Wilfrid Andrews basked in congratulations. How marvellous that he had persuaded the BBC to give the race major radio coverage that afternoon! What a lovely map of the circuit there had been in this week's *Radio Times*! And the race itself was one of the five 'Highlights of the

The Control Tower, as converted by the BRDC for its current practical use (*above*), with four of its guests in 1948 (*right*).

Week' on its cover! To be ranked with Gracie Fields, the Brains Trust, Bernard Shaw's *St Joan* and the Vienna Philharmonic Orchestra was really something!

There was inevitably some chatter, too, about Lord Howe. Wasn't that his latest wife with him, looking so smart and charming? Was she number three or number four? And hadn't he been through a rather turbulent time in other matters too? There was talk of Penn House, his old family home, being requisitioned in the war, used by a prep school and mistreated so badly it was still not habitable. Where was he living these days with his stable of lovely cars? In an old Surrey rectory? Apparently the new Countess Howe would be presenting the victor with his laurels at the end. What a brick she must be! But wouldn't Wilfrid Andrews have been more appropriate, as he had organised the whole Grand Prix?

As the happy party broke up, Wilfrid Andrews was beaming. His own insistence on wines of a good vintage had been felicitous. Samuelson's plonk would have let down the whole show. The guests were excitedly crossing the footbridge and finding their seats, as the ladies of Silverstone started the clearing up around Capt. Bolton.

* * *

Rodney Walkerley's distorted voice, giving a résumé of the final preparations, floated across the aerodrome from the battery of loudspeakers, as he juggled inside his little hut with hastily scribbled pieces of information. There had been much last-minute changing of plugs, the ERAs had been on jacks as they had their pre-selective gearboxes warmed up, and all the teams were suddenly frantically busy. Chiron and the Ecurie France, up at the far end, were typical. They'd apparently been trying to install a bottle on the dashboard so Chiron could have a drink during the race. A good idea, but lack of time would probably defeat them. Chiron's rev counter, meanwhile, seemed not to be working. His mechanics had rushed towards Lord Selsdon's Talbot but this was a different model. The rev counters were dissimilar. Chiron, however, remained unconcernedly smiling. '*Pas de problème*! I'll just have to trust my ears!'

Another scrap of paper, urgently thrust into Rodney Walkerley's hand, stopped the anecdotal flow.

Well, ladies and gentlemen, prepare yourselves for a treat! The cars are coming out onto the track on their way to the grid.

Alan Hess, who was leading the BBC's commentary team, was already perched 20 feet up on a platform of scaffolding by the central intersection. Even though the sun was out, the October winds, sweeping across the flat airfield, seemed distinctly chilly and sudden gusts were constantly threatening to sweep away his papers. Forty-eight-years-old, with a strikingly ample figure and bald head, Hess was the BBC's most experienced commentator in motor sport. He had known Brooklands as competitor, entrant and promoter, been the founder editor of *Speed* (the BRDC's magazine, later subsumed by *Motor Sport*) and was currently managing the Austin Motor Company's promotions department, where he was forever inventing spectacular record-breaking events in which he himself would usually participate. His recent book, *Gullible's Travels*, told how three Austin Sixteens visited seven European capitals in seven days.

Hess's colleague, thirty-three-year-old Max Robertson, down at the start-finish area, had this year covered Wimbledon, the

London Olympics and the Winter Olympics at St Moritz, where he had given a running commentary as a passenger on the British bobsleigh team as they roared down the Cresta Run. Motor racing, however, was not his forte, and he'd been very surprised to be sent to Silverstone. 'Presumably they thought that if I had the speed for Wimbledon I should be all right for motor racing. Nothing really could have been further from the truth.' He was completely unmechanical, totally untechnical, hated noise and found 'the fumes generated by a pack of racing cars quite unpalatable'.

The race had been given three live sessions on the Light Programme that together would last almost a third of the projected race time of three hours. The race would be following some of Britain's favourite radio programmes: *Housewives' Choice*; the hour-long omnibus edition of *Dick Barton, Special Agent*; Winifred Atwell's *Piano Playtime*; and organist Reginald Dixon *At The Console*, live from the Tower Ballroom, Blackpool.

As the cars made their way to the grid, Hess saw them twice: first, as they streamed down the runway to the Segrave hairpin before turning left for Maggot's; then, secondly, coming back from the other end of the same runway, before rounding Seaman and heading towards Club. Hess, therefore, had a grandstand view of the one great flaw in the design of the circuit: cars approaching each other head-on from opposite directions. Complaints after practice had led to Jimmy Brown erecting some canvas screens to mask the view, but there were still only 80 yards of tarmac and a few straw bales separating Segrave from Seaman.

* * *

Rodney Walkerley no longer needed scraps of paper. He had twenty-five cars on the grid in front of him. Parnell's Maserati had a puddle of fuel at its rear, the result of over-enthusiastic last-minute topping-up. Harrison's ERA was having a frantic warm-up on the jack, but seemed OK. De Graffenried's mechanics were delving deep into the recesses of the Maserati's engine department…

* * *

Gigi Villoresi was standing beside his Maserati, shirt sleeves rolled up at the elbows, chatting to a young mechanic. He and Alberto had enjoyed a good evening in Northampton. It wasn't exactly a sophisticated place. But the older part of the town had a certain quaint provincial charm, and they had enjoyed a convivial time at the Angel Hotel.

Starting a race from the very back row was a novelty, not least after being on the front row at his last three Grands Prix. And with no Alfas to worry about, there was something quite amusing about the situation. They'd been placed on the pits' side of the track, but both he and Alberto intended to accelerate out to the left, using the great width of the road and avoiding being hemmed in.

Alberto, on his immediate left, was already in his Maserati and lost in thought. Bertocchi was fussing around both cars, but seemingly more out of habit than intent. As Gigi buttoned up his white linen head covering, he wandered forward and exchanged encouraging grins with George Nixon and Bob Ansell. It was good to remind them just who and what was behind them.

* * *

Max Robertson rushed out of his little commentary box near the start-line in frustration. More and more people were gathering in front of it, seemingly oblivious of his situation. The blaring noise coming from the loudspeakers – a mixture of Rodney Walkerley and rampant oscillation – was combining with many a revving engine to drown his pleas completely. And there was no time for any more. With the race about to start he just had to be back at the microphone…

* * *

Reginald Dixon had bid the nation a fond farewell with 'I Do Like To Be Beside The Seaside', and it was 'over to Alan Hess at Silverstone Aerodrome'. Hess knew he had up to ten minutes before handing over to Robertson at the start, but was in an expansive mood. He was only halfway through the list of entrants and had not yet mentioned the grid when he was shocked to be taken out by Robertson. The young whipper-snapper had just about as much knowledge of racing cars as his Aunt Fanny. But at least Hess could gulp down a glass of champagne in a silent toast to his good friend Lord Howe at his moment of triumph.

The race programme's list of entries for the Grand Prix with a spectator's attempts to keep track of the early part of the race.

R.A.C. Grand Prix 1948

NO.	CAR	ENTRANT	DRIVER	RESERVE DRIVER	NO. OF CYLS.	C.C.
1	Talbot	Ecurie France	Louis Chiron	—	6	4500
2	Talbot	G. Comotti	G. Comotti	—	6	4500
3	Talbot	L. Rosier	L. Rosier	—	6	4500
4	Talbot	P. Etancelin	P. Etancelin	—	6	4500
5	Talbot (R)	Lord Selsdon	Lord Selsdon	Lord Waleran	6	4500
6	Maserati	R. Parnell	R. Parnell	—	4	1496 (S)
7	Maserati (R)	F. Ashmore	F. Ashmore	D. Murray	4	1496 (S)
8	Maserati	D. Hamilton	D. Hamilton	—	6	1496 (S)
9	Maserati	R. E. Ansell	R. E. Ansell	G. H. Bainbridge	4	1496 (S)
10	Ferrari	R. Sommer	R. Sommer	—	12	1497 (S)
11	Ferrari	G. Farina	G. Farina	—	12	1497 (S)
12	E.R.A.	Raymond Mays	Raymond Mays	W. K. Richardson	6	1488 (S)
14	E.R.A. (E. Type)	P. D. C. Walker	P. D. C. Walker	—	6	1487 (S)
15	E.R.A. (E. Type)	Leslie Johnson	Leslie Johnson	—	6	1487 (S)
16	E.R.A.	F. R. Gerard	F. R. Gerard	—	6	1488 (S)
17	Alta (R)	G. Watson	G. Watson	—	4	1491 (S)
18	Maserati	Scuderia Ambrosiana	L. Villoresi	—	4	1496 (S)
19	Maserati	H.R.H. Prince Chula	" B. Bira "	—	4	1496 (S)
20	Maserati	E. Platé	Baron de Graffenried	E. Platé	4	1496 (S)
21	Maserati (R)	A. A. Baring	A. A. Baring	—	6	1496 (S)
22	E.R.A.	G. Ansell	G. Ansell	B. Shawe-Taylor	6	1488 (S)
23	E.R.A.	T. C. Harrison	T. C. Harrison	—	6	1488 (S)
24	E.R.A.	D. A. Hampshire	D. A. Hampshire	P. Fotheringham-Parker	6	1488 (S)
25	E.R.A. (R)	P. H. Bell	J. V. Bolster	—	6	1488 (S)
26	Maserati	S. J. Gilbey	S. J. Gilbey	—	6	1496 (S)
27	Maserati	Rowland Motors, Ltd.	R. F. Salvadori	—	4	1496 (S)
28	Maserati	Alfieri Maserati	H. L. Brooke	—	4	1496 (S)
29	Alfa-Romeo	A. P. R. Rolt	A. P. R. Rolt	—	8	3442
30	E.R.A. (R)	G. Nixon	G. Nixon	—	6	1488 (S)
31	E.R.A.—Riley (R)	G. Richardson	G. Richardson	—	6	1488 (S)
32	Emeryson	R. Baird	R. Baird	P. R. Emery	8	4350

(R) = Denotes Reserve Entry.
(S) = Denotes Supercharged Engine.
c.c. = Denotes Cubic Capacity of Engine.

12

CHAPTER 12

Max Robertson now rather wished he hadn't taken Alan Hess out. He had missed Lord Howe letting down his Union Jack with the finest of flourishes. Indeed, he only had a vague idea that a flash of red meant that de Graffenried had led the front row for the first few yards, for his only secure view was of the roof of the grandstand and the hoardings on the footbridge advertising *The Motor*. He was rather stuck, rapidly running out of inappropriate generalisations like 'the flag is up – they're off'. It was a merciful relief when Alan Hess took him out rather quicker than had been agreed.

* * *

Reg Parnell had out-accelerated the rest of the second row at the start and was willing a gap to open up in front of him between Chiron's Talbot and de Graffenried's Maserati. It didn't. De Graffenried had got away amazingly well and was leading the race, but Chiron was not far behind him. No gap there! This initial surge had taken Parnell past the slow-starting Étancelin and as they settled down, speeding between the second grandstand and the line of pits on the approach to the first right-hander, Woodcote, Parnell was right up the back of Chiron and had left de Graffenried trailing in his wake. Gerard too had disappeared, having got off the line quite slowly. To

Parnell's left, on the far outside, there was the green E-type of Leslie Johnson who had recovered from a poor start, but, in following Chiron Parnell was taking the tight line through the right-hander. Poor old Leslie would have to stay on the outside and go the long way round!

Reg was surprised by Chiron's evident pace down the short straight to Copse. He knew he was quicker than Étancelin and the other Talbots, but Chiron's new car certainly was a flier. A green blur on his left, momentarily eclipsing the massed spectators lining this side of the track, meant Leslie Johnson was looking to take him under braking for the coming right-hander – and in the very E-type that he himself had sold back to Leslie at the beginning of the year! After all the trouble he'd had with it and all the abortive developments he'd given it, dear old Leslie was surely not going to make a winner of it, was he? He moved across, very close to the E-type. Copse was a corner to respect. As they turned sharply off the perimeter road and onto the longest of the runways – a full 120 degrees – it was easy to miss the breaking, crash through the oil drums and slide out disastrously wide. But he still left his braking late. Johnson backed off, and Parnell followed Chiron through the ever-tightening right-hander. Thanks to the oil drums, the track was surprisingly narrow at

The start (1): Lord Howe (*left*) watches as Chiron, de Graffenried, Étancelin and Gerard blast away from the front row. Parnell, in the second row, looks vainly for a gap between Chiron and de Graffenried, with a lagging Bira on his right and Walker and Rolt to his left. (*Guy Griffiths Collection*)

The start (2): A Grandstand spectator's view of de Graffenried's Maserati leading off the line, with Gerard's ERA on the right.

The start (3): Bira (19) leads the third row – Harrison (23), Comotti (2), Rosier (3) and Bolster (25) – under the footbridge. The rest of the first two rows are out of sight. (*Guy Griffiths Collection*)

the apex and it was only as the line of drums opened out that the full width of the runway from Copse asserted itself, and its length, too, stretching out as far as the eye could see.

Chiron was easing away from him and Leslie Johnson's E-type was alongside briefly, then pulling ahead. Its top speed down the half-mile straight – over 150 mph – outdid Parnell's new Maserati, but only for a while. Halfway down, foot to the floor, Parnell expected to see the E-type grow elusively smaller. Instead, he flashed past it as the E-type slowed and he only just managed to scrub off his speed for the left-hand hairpin where the runways intersected. What had happened to Leslie? He couldn't see him in his mirrors as he accelerated towards another tight bend, this time the right-hander at Maggot's that brought him back to the perimeter road. Soon he was following Chiron

through the curves at Becket's and Chapel before chasing him down towards Stowe, with two black hangars on his left.

The crowd had vanished since Chapel. No crowd now. No spectators were allowed on the outside of Stowe (one of the many sharp right-handers) and of course the Stowe-Copse runway was eerily empty as it led back to the central intersection. No crowd there, either, except a few photographers, a couple of commentators on high perches, a movie camera on top of a van and a few parked cars and hangers-on. It was the oddest thing about this new circuit. Half of it was packed with spectators and half of it almost totally empty. As he turned left at Seaman and headed down the runway to Club, all was still desolation. He had two blue cars in his mirrors – Étancelin and Bira, in all probability. It was unlikely that Rosier or Comotti were going

Étancelin leads Bira.
(*Guy Griffiths Collection*)

that well. It was a pleasure to be rounding Club, for though it was yet another irritatingly slow right-hander, the crowd was back again, a sudden mass of humanity in Enclosure A. As he swung up towards Abbey, with Chiron some 50 yards ahead and Étancelin a little less behind, he felt suddenly confident. After so many years of driving fairly elderly machinery, Reg had at last worked himself to a position where he could expect good results on a regular basis. At least, once Wilkie Wilkinson had fully sorted the car. As photographers wandered down the side of the track towards him, he swept up the hill and under the footbridge. It was going to be a long race, and Chiron's new car, even more unsorted than his own, must surely be suspect.

* * *

Bill Boddy was soon learning from the disappointed Leslie Johnson the cause of his retirement on the very first lap. He had been up there fighting for the lead with Chiron, when, with a crash and a jerk, a universal joint had broken and the half-shaft flown free. He had 'zig-zagged' the car to free the axle and braked as hard as he could, but the flailing half-shaft had torn a hole in the fuel tank before banging up and down along the tarmac, leaving a trail of sparks. The torrents of petrol escaping from the tank had duly exploded, leaving a ball of flame behind. John Bolster had gone right through it and nearly crashed into Johnson's stricken ERA.

Villoresi comes out of Club as he works his way through the field. It is too early in the race for the RAC's scoreboard (facing the Members' enclosure) to have any car numbers displayed. (*Guy Griffiths Collection*)

Halfway down the longest runway, Bob Gerard enters Segrave. (*Guy Griffiths Collection*)

* * *

Guy Griffiths, having watched the start from the pits, had crossed the footbridge and wandered down the road to Abbey. Chiron and Parnell had already passed but he captured Étancelin and Bira, close together in third and fouth. Comotti was up to 5th; and de Graffenried and Gerard, though demoted from their front row positions as expected, were sixth and seventh, still keeping ahead of Rosier. To Guy's surprise, Ascari and Villoresi were already in eigth and ninth and closing in on all three as they headed up to the starting line. Nixon and Gilbey were duelling at the tail of the long train of cars, with Mays behind, having a race by himself after stalling on the grid. As yet, there was no sign of Salvadori.

* * *

Raymond Mays, at the rear of the field, was too experienced to be demoralised. A three-hour race was one of attrition. Many of the drivers ahead of him had scant experience of racing in any form, let alone in an endurance event like this. So he pressed on determinedly, though aware that his faithful ERA was strangely off-form. The size of the crowd surprised him and so too the way it had improved the feel of the old airfield. Silverstone's broad acres impressed him. The site had definite potential and could be a boost to the BRM's development process. His anxieties about the project had relaxed a little after a few days with friends in the civilised atmosphere of Stratford-upon-Avon. And there had been so much excitement about the opening of the circuit that those intent on harassing him had been distracted.

Opposite: Tony Rolt's Alfa Romeo leads Cuth Harrison and David Hampshire through Club. (*Guy Griffiths Collection*)

Inset: Gordon Watson and Bob Ansell approach Abbey. (*Guy Griffiths Collection*)

Perhaps one day a BRM might be leading a Grand Prix here? With himself at the wheel? It was a possibility, but no more. He needed to show he was as quick as ever. It was time to regather his concentration and press on determinedly…

* * *

Gigi was enjoying himself. Alberto had beaten him off the line and swept by the slow-starting Sam Gilbey. He had swiftly followed, passing on the right of Gilbey before moving left, close to the grass verge, full of officials, and easing past three of the other back-markers before he had even passed the second hangar. Alberto, by contrast, had chosen to move back to the centre where his meteoric progress was slowed. Gigi was almost adjacent to Alberto as they entered Woodcote. Fast corners were always great fun. He had taken an immediate liking to

Woodcote, fast enough to show off the Maserati's road-holding, the tail sliding, but delicately so, always under his complete control. Copse was far too tight for his liking, but the work done recently on the brakes paid off here as it would do on all the other similarly slow corners. The blast down Segrave Straight was an odd sensation to someone who loved racing on public roads in sun-kissed Mediterranean cities packed with admiring *tifosi*. The funnelling by oil drums into the left-hander at the intersection seemed a clumsy device. Functional but inelegant. That was the British temperament, lacking all finesse. They were earnest and well-intentioned, hard-working and brave. He liked them a lot. But finesse? *Niente*!

Gigi had hardly noticed whom he'd passed. He was simply following Alberto. It must have been half the field by the first

Peter Walker leads Bira and Chiron up the first half of the Stowe-Copse runway, lining up the left-hander at the central intersection. (*Guy Griffiths Collection*)

The same three cars go round the left-hander at the intersection, before heading down the runway to Club. In the background, one of several mobile newsreel teams. (*Guy Griffiths Collection*)

time they reached the end of Hangar Straight and began the runway to Seaman. He had known Dick Seaman well – not, perhaps, the most *simpatico* of Englishmen. They were near contemporaries, but he had found him *un poco lontano* – aloof. He had done well for Mercedes, of course, before tragically overreaching himself at Spa. How touching that the British should honour his memory. Would he himself be ever honoured like that? Or Alberto?

* * *

Reg Parnell was determined to pass Chiron. If he could pass Chiron, then he could finish the race in third, for he had no illusions about the Italians. They had clearly ensured that the 4CLT he had collected at Modena for the race at Turin was no match for the Ambrosiana cars. It was perfectly understandable. He would have done the same in their position. It was all part of getting an advantage over one's rivals. What motor racing was all about? And with the admirable Wilkie Wilkinson working for him, he had the opportunity of beating them at their own game in the longer term.

Chiron was still a frustrating 30 yards ahead, as Parnell entered Copse, a little faster than usual, for the second time. He was neatly close to the oil drums on the corner's tight apex, but then found himself drifting out rather wider than he had intended and was sliding towards one of the old aerodrome landing lights protruding above the tarmac. The noise underneath the Maserati was sickening. So, too, the rich smell of petrol. The tank's drain plug must have been ripped out by the impact and, as a result, he was losing petrol fast. It was going to be a long walk back to the pits.

* * *

Alan Hess guffawed and took out Max Robertson. The young whipper-snapper had just called Ascari's Maserati 'Farina's Ferrari'! No, even worse – 'Ferrari's Farina'! The listeners would be somewhat perplexed. What Max had done, of course, in a moment of panic about identifying one of the red cars, was to consult his programme, and there No. 11 was, indeed, Farina in a Ferrari. But honestly! Surely everyone present that afternoon knew that Ascari was a late race entry and had taken over the absent Farina's number? But not Max, when in a panic!

Time was running out for this first transmission. They would be handing back to the studio at 2.10 p.m., for there was no possibility that the BBC would move their regular Saturday afternoon discussion programme *New and Old Books*. And they would not be back on air for another eighty minutes, for there was also the immovable Rae Jenkins and the BBC Variety Orchestra's *Band Call*. It was important, then, to put the listeners fully in the picture before the big break. The rapid progress of Villoresi and Ascari was his major concern, with Villoresi putting in a record lap of 76.12 mph. But Parnell's demise was another thing he should mention and he'd just received a helpful note about his losing all his petrol. Fancy that, he told the listeners, with a smile. Reg had lost all his petrol! And the government had only just restored the basic ration. Would this mean that the Minister of Fuel, Mr Hugh Gaitskell, would remove it again? What was it that Mr Gaitskell had said last January, when removing the basic ration? 'It'll save us 40 million dollars and allow us to buy all the lard we need to provide the whole of our cooking fat ration?' Reg couldn't have lost all that much, of course, not all of Mr Gaitskell's 40 million dollars' worth. Listeners could surely rest content that Mr Gaitskell wasn't going to have to step in again and secure the lard supply.

Ascari leads Villoresi through Abbey. (*Guy Griffiths Collection*)

And so the first broadcast had ended, with him talking of lard rather than motor racing. The more Hess had tried to extract himself from the diversion about Gaitskell and petrol rationing, the deeper he had got into it. He knew the digression would probably mean letters from Outraged of Purley and Disgusted of Dorking. So thank goodness for Ferrari's Farina! With a bit of luck Max's error would draw some of the fire in next week's *Motor*…

* * *

Bill Boddy, noting down Parnell's absence, looked up in time to see Chiron swoop by at the start of lap 3, with a lead of 100 yards over Étancelin and Bira, but with Ascari and Villoresi closing in, much nearer now, in fourth and fifth. Comotti, sixth, was dropping back, and came in at the end of the third lap with brake problems. The Talbot's bonnet was duly lifted, the front wheels jacked up, and the nearside brake adjusted. All this time Comotti remained in the cockpit, but with a look on his face which clearly and correctly suggested that the car's race was run. He had been second at Albi and fourth at Reims, but this was his third and most disappointing retirement of the season. He had felt at home in England and so too his glamorous wife. Indeed, his hotel bill and other considerable expenses would only come second to de Graffenried's. Franco Comotti had liked everything about his trip and had very much hoped to put on a good show. But *che sarà, sarà*.

* * *

Rodney Walkerley, from his vantage point on the potato fields above the start line, made the most on the PA of the change of lead, as the fourth lap began. Not only had the two Maseratis overtaken Chiron, with Villoresi putting in another record lap time (of 77.73 mph, just 2 minutes 50 seconds), but they were leaving him behind. A little later, Walkerley began his first summary: the race was now settling down into three clear sections. First, the gleaming red Maseratis of Villoresi and Ascari, jousting gently together, often travelling side by side, changing gear as one. Secondly, strung out well behind, the other foreign challengers: Chiron, some sixteen seconds behind the leaders; Bira, steadily getting faster, but still fourteen seconds behind Chiron; Étancelin, six seconds behind Bira; and Rosier and de Graffenried, occasionally swapping places. Then, and only then, came the best of the British. Walkerley spoke regretfully. The two best English hopes, Parnell and Johnson, were already out of the race, and that left only cars that were thoroughly outclassed, a dozen or so years old, kept racing by the devoted administrations of their owners. Even the leader, Bob Gerard, whose ERA was always superbly prepared, was having to content himself with sitting back in eighth place. But it was a long race. They must not get too despondent. Bob Gerard's time might yet come…

It was not long before there were four more disappointed British drivers. Only ten minutes into the race, Gordon Watson had abandoned his unreliable Alta on the grass near the intersection with a leaking petrol tank. Having rushed back to the pits, he had returned with a set of tools and gallantly managed to restart, seemingly having solved his problem, only to stop again out on the circuit and push the Alta onto the grass verge, where it remained with what turned out to be a sheared camshaft drive. Tony Rolt's Alfa had lasted six laps in a midfield position before its engine gave up on him. Duncan Hamilton survived only two laps longer, but he had already delighted watchers with 'several exhibitions of undue zeal', causing

Duncan Hamilton's Maserati enters Segrave Corner, having come down the Segrave Straight from Copse. A photographer prepares to cross the main runway. (*Guy Griffiths Collection*)

Enclosure A at Club Corner particular excitement when his elderly Maserati spun and knocked over three marker barrels. Having lost all his oil pressure, Hamilton returned to the pits on the pillion of one of the many helpful RAC motorcyclists. The young Geoff Richardson, meanwhile, who had been going well in his ERA-Riley and was not too far detached from the battle of the leading British, was the other early retirement, pushed into the pits with rear axle failure.

Bill Boddy was on hand in the Lago-Talbot pits when Étancelin, running fifth, unexpectedly called in with overheating: 'A board was set to indicate the stopping position at Étancelin's pit, and, as the Talbot slithered in, can after can of water went into the radiator, Étancelin sucking at half an orange and not seeing his wife's desire that he should accept fresh gloves. He stalled in restarting, then roared back into the fray.' But he was now at the back of the leading group of pre-war cars, headed by Bob Gerard, who was being followed by Cuth Harrison, Toulo de Graffenried in his overheating Maserati, David Hampshire, Peter Walker, Geoffrey Ansell and John Bolster.

The older cars were mostly having a difficult race. George Nixon's ERA lost a minute having the front wheels changed. Bob Ansell's Maserati, trailing oil, had spun at Seaman Corner and hit the straw bales at Becket's, where it badly dented its nose, Ansell being forced to make a pitstop to remove straw from his boiling radiator. Salvadori was going steadily after his early problems, but was amazed at the speed differential every time the leading Maseratis went rushing past him. Raymond Mays, after a steady drive had brought him to the rear of the battle of backmarkers, had been forced on lap 10 to stop for a plug change. Worse, during refuelling almost the whole contents of

the third churn were somehow poured over the back of the car, and some frantic mopping up delayed him further. Eventually, he was push-started back into the race, yet again at the very tail of the field.

* * *

By lap 12, by contrast, Gigi and Alberto were having a terrific time, enlivening the race for themselves and the spectators. Gigi had taken the lead as soon as they had passed Chiron, but after three laps he had let Alberto slip by. Two laps further, he had retaken the lead, only for Alberto to pass him next lap and then, two laps later, he had re-passed Alberto on the outside of Woodcote. He could sense the spectators' excitement and imagine the smile on Alberto's lips. Bertocchi in the Ambrosiana pits was probably the only person at Silverstone not particularly enjoying himself.

For an experienced driver, the course was not taxing, the only problem being the immense amount of oil being spilt by the most elderly cars, which, without catch tanks, automatically blew oil from their breathers onto the track. But it was just a case of keeping alert at the trouble spots; he could relax elsewhere. It was hard not to let the thoughts wander when there was so little sense of imminent danger; danger, of course, had been what had alarmed his dear father when he and his brother Emilio were starting out. Papa and Mamma had understood their joint passion but shared a real fear of it. Papa, of course, had never driven a car, preferring to employ a succession of chauffeurs for the large limousines that befitted his position in Milan. What subterfuges and lies Gigi had had to adopt to be able to use one of his father's cars in his earliest events! On one occasion, when he had taken out a seven-seat Lancia Lambda to do a hill-climb

The fierce battle between Geoffrey Ansell (22) and John Bolster (25), which was to end abruptly at Maggot's shortly afterwards. (*Guy Griffiths Collection*)

up Monte Presolana, he had ended up with half the car balancing over a huge drop! But his dear father had never known.

Gigi was approaching the tight Seaman Corner for the twelfth time, unaware of a new deposit of oil from Bob Ansell's Maserati. A miscalculation now found him sliding out of control towards the oil drums at the outside of the corner and further and further from the apex he had intended to clip. By good luck he missed the drums, and though he hit the hay bales with some force, the Maserati, with its low centre of gravity, did not overturn. By the time he had extricated himself from all the hay and found a gear, Alberto had passed and was disappearing down the runway towards Club. Gigi, furious with himself but relieved he hadn't stalled, gave pursuit. Alberto would surely dine off this for weeks.

By lap 15 he had caught Alberto and overtaken him. Gigi relaxed again and within seconds Alberto slipped by. Gigi, restored to good humour, stayed right on his tail.

* * *

Max Robertson by the start-line had long since persuaded the crowd obstructing his view to move away and was conscientiously making notes of the changing lead for the next broadcast: Villoresi lap 18; Ascari lap 20; Villoresi lap 22; Ascari lap 23. Both cars by then were a minute and a half ahead of Bira in his royal blue Maserati. Bira himself was just ahead of Chiron. There was a certain interest, Max had to admit, in the grim relentlessness of it all, but it really wasn't like Centre Court…

* * *

As he passed the pits each lap, Philippe Étancelin, with the peak of his cap facing backwards as usual, was regretting that he had turned down his wife's suggestion of sunglasses and was having to drive one-handed, shielding his eyes from the sun. The car was still overheating and he was making no impression on the middle of the field. Bill Boddy was close at hand when, on lap 23, the Frenchman came in for what would be the last of several pitstops. Almost as quickly as the mechanics poured water into the radiator, it came to the boil. A cracked cylinder head resulted. 'Étancelin had a drink,' noted Boddy. 'Comotti talked with him, then the car was retired, the driver changing his cap for a clean one, donning a wonderful tweed sports coat, and resigning himself to watching from the pit counter.' His wife gave him a consoling hug; Paul Vallée a consoling glass of brandy.

* * *

John Bolster, enjoying his mid-life elevation from hill-climb specialist to Grand Prix driver and handling his green ERA with characteristic exuberance, had been having a long battle with Geoffrey Ansell's blue ERA towards the back of the midfield. There was little performance difference between the two cars. Bolster was the more experienced, but Ansell had gained confidence from a recent victory on the Isle of Man and was holding Bolster's challenge off with some panache. Bolster, rightly believing his brakes were now the stronger, was becoming more and more speculative. Eventually, on lap 23, he made his move to overtake Ansell on the inside going into Maggot's, a 90 degree right-hander linking the Club-Maggot's runway to the perimeter road. Ansell duly went into the corner on the outside, intent on getting a faster exit. Instead, however, he slid wide, touched some straw bales on the grass verge and instantly overturned.

Most of the photographers, like Guy Griffiths, were limiting themselves to the intersection and the area between Club and the pits, but Dennis Oulds, a thirty-one-year-old from Central

Villoresi (8) and Ascari joust with each other as they round Segrave. In the background can be discerned, behind the crops, a Nissen hut belonging to the farm, paddock marquees, the Control Tower and a well-established line of apple trees. (*Guy Griffiths Collection*)

Press, had come out to the far side of the circuit to try to capture something a little different. He had been an official photographer during the war, witnessing battles like the crossing of the Rhine, yet as he stood on the grass verge outside Maggot's that afternoon he would have struggled to think of anything more immediately appalling than Ansell's ERA approaching him at 70 mph, broadside on, front wheels sliding along a row of straw bales, back wheels skidding along the tarmac, about to overturn in the exact spot where he was standing. He took his photograph and jumped. Over his shoulder he caught sight of a moving blur as the flying car, turning tail-to-front at the same time that it was rolling over, bounced three times in a dense cloud of soil, straw and smoke, only ejecting Ansell after the second bounce, before coming to a standstill, right way up, in a thick haze. Miraculously, it had rolled parallel to the massed crowds of Enclosure E, 20 yards away, rather than into them. Miraculously, too, Ansell seemed only to have an injured ankle.

Reports played down the incident. The official race bulletin, issued at intervals to the press, stated: '3.11 p.m.: G. Ansell overturned at Maggot's Corner. The driver is only shaken and has become a spectator.' Bill Boddy later gave *Motor Sport* readers further details: 'Ansell bravely refused the ambulance, although his right leg was injured, his fingers cut, and he nearly fainted from shock.' Soon afterwards Bob Ansell, having entrusted his Maserati to co-driver George Bainbridge, went to see how his cousin was. He and his wife later drove the shaken Geoffrey back to his Hampshire home. Dennis Oulds, meanwhile, decided that he had taken enough photographs for one day. He had never much enjoyed motor sport, anyway. Cricket was his passion and nothing had happened that afternoon to change that preference.

* * *

Gigi was relieved to see that all seemed well at Maggot's and delighted when the good Bertocchi indicated that he and Alberto were now a minute and three-quarters ahead of Bira. His pits had also indicated it was time to make the first stop: *Prossimo Giro: BOX*. Alberto was currently in the lead, but Gigi had almost drawn level as they came under the bridge, before swooping to the right, braking hard for the pits and at the same time turning off his engine. '82 minutes: Car 18's first stop,' noted Max Robertson, not far away. He replaced his headphones. In another eight minutes, he and Alan Hess would be starting their second stint.

Bill Boddy was not going to miss the Ambrosiana pitstops. 'Immense anticipation as Villoresi was expected for refuelling! The Maserati came in, the driver dirty and excited, Villoresi leapt out, wiped his goggles and leapt back in, the fuel going in under pressure, without a hitch. Pumping with his right hand, Villoresi was push-started, and the stop cost but 35.6 seconds, the crowd clapping appreciatively.' Refuelling with a pressure hose, noted Boddy, was a distinct advantage over the churns and funnels used elsewhere, with human error virtually eliminated. The Italians could deliver 30 gallons in just ten seconds.

Boddy was still there two laps later when Ascari came in: 'He stayed in the cockpit, watching impatiently as rear wheels were changed and the fuel put in, also oil and water. Then he caught sight of a mechanic holding a cloth, wiped his goggles, the jack was released, and the car was away – 1 minute 27 seconds with only two men on the job.' But why did Ascari need new rear wheels? Tyres, as distinct from tyre pressures, were not a big issue for any car that afternoon. Why did Ascari have his Pirellis

Geoffrey Ansell loses his ERA on the exit to Maggot's. (*Getty Images*)

changed? The Maserati was clearly working perfectly during its first stint. Changing the wheels cost him time he would be unable to make up. It seems that Guarino Bertocchi had made a unilateral decision (of modern resonance) that his two cars would not throw the race away by taking each other out. Gigi was to win. In the circumstances, it was quite understandable that Alberto had shown 'impatience' as the wheels were changed.

* * *

Gigi was disappointed. Where was Alberto? Even on the longest straights there was no sign of Italian red in his mirrors. He shrugged his shoulders questioningly as he passed Bertocchi in the pits. *Niente*! Bertocchi seemed not to have noticed. He shrugged again. Still no reaction. He swooped angrily close to the pits for the third time and screamed his question above the engine noise. '*Dov'è Alberto?*' Bertocchi merely shook his fist. There was no sign of a crash around the circuit. '*Dov'è Alberto*'? At 40 laps, Bertocchi held out a sign: '50 sec. Alberto'. Nearly a minute behind! He

could slow down, of course, and let his friend catch up. But if he surrendered the best part of a minute and then the car started playing up, he would look very foolish. *Va bene*. He must settle down and concentrate. He mustn't doze off on the runways.

* * *

Below: George Nixon makes a pit stop. The farm building visible behind still stands.

Opposite: Villoresi hurries onto the main runway at Copse, well in the lead. The spectators in D Enclosure, watching him from the airfield's perimeter road (which in 1949 would be incorporated into the circuit), paid only £1 per car because they were so far away from the action. (*Revs Institute for Automotive Research*)

Alan Hess, with eighty minutes to kill before the next broadcast, could hardly be blamed if he exchanged his windy perch for the nearest refreshment marquee. When 3.10 p.m. arrived and it was 'over to Alan Hess at Silverstone Aerodrome', he was in a comfortably benign mood, happy to let the youthful Max have a fling. The ninny was hardly likely to spot any more Ferraris at this stage of the race, and it would do him good to earn his fee. Besides, Alan seemed to have mislaid that pile of information sheets from race control...

A professional summary duly followed from Max Robertson: Ascari had endured a long pitstop and was well behind Villoresi. He had also lost his exhaust pipe, which fortunately hadn't struck the lapped, but closely following John Bolster. Louis Chiron had repassed Bira, who had serious brake problems, before Chiron himself had been in the pits with handling troubles and, with Bira, had dropped right back. That meant, then, that British hopes were rising for Gerard, who had yet to stop and was now fourth. Louis Rosier, whose Talbot wasn't expected to have to refuel at all, was third.

By the time the twenty-minute broadcast ended, the race was but half over. Twenty minutes was hardly generous, but Saturday afternoon was the traditional time for the second half of a First Division football match. And so, at 3.50 p.m., it was goodbye from Alan Hess and Max Robertson at Silverstone and welcome to the Molyneux ground, Wolverhampton, where Wolves, captained by Billy Wright, were playing another top team, Huddersfield Town.

* * *

Bill Boddy had witnessed from the Ecurie France pits Chiron's stop for handling problems, which lost him forty-five seconds and dropped him from third to sixth. He had also witnessed several subsequent episodes of Gallic temperament. At the first stop, an extremely animated and noisy one, Chiron had expressed his outrage at the tail-happy behaviour of his Lago-Talbot. This led eventually to a change in tyre pressures, and with over 50lb in the back tyres he had gone out again, giving a thumbs-up sign as he first passed. This, however, soon changed, for several laps, to a shaking of the fist and a pointing to the tyres, before a second stop that found Chiron even more agitated. As he climbed out of the car, he was already yelling at his mechanics (fortunately in French) hostile phrases like '*Merde, bande de salauds*' and demanding to see the French Dunlop representative, that archetypal *salaud*. The poor rep was duly found and given a furious lecture, not entirely free of strong expressions. The rep, however, responded very mildly – he clearly knew his man – and this seemed to disappoint Chiron, who turned his anger on the mechanics over tyre pressures and the rear suspension. Eventually, the rear Dunlops were changed at his request, though they had plenty of tread left, and off again went Chiron with rather more applause from the grandstand than the pits. Very soon, however, on lap 39, he stopped out on the course with oil pouring from underneath the car and stalked away to retire. A bottle of Hennessey brandy, tactfully supplied by the delightful Madame Étancelin, briefly fortified the spirits of Paul Vallée and his silk-clad mechanics, but they managed to put on long faces of remorse when Chiron suddenly appeared to curse resoundingly both the gearbox and those who had ministered to it. How could a brand new gearbox have seized solid like that? He really was not at all impressed with this new Lago-Talbot! It had clearly been put together by *salauds*! No-one dared mention that he had been changing gear without a rev counter and perhaps his wonderful ear had let him down.

Mays at Club, attempting to redeem his poor start.

A wonderfully vivid Michael Turner painting of Bob Gerard at Maggot's in front of Bira, Rosier and the two Ambrosiana Maseratis. (*Courtesy of Michael Turner*)

CHAPTER 13

Soon after half distance, there were several further British retirements. Raymond Mays knew by the time of a second pitstop on lap 35 that he had serious engine problems, and though he put on a show for the grandstand crowd by accelerating away with spinning wheels, he returned one lap later to retire with a broken piston. Sam Gilbey had a shambolic pitstop in which large quantities of fuel were poured down his back instead of into his old Maserati. His Welsh co-driver, Dudley Folland, quickly took over, but even the grit that had served Folland well as a wartime Army officer could not prevail – unlike Villoresi, Folland had been on the winning side at Tripoli – and on lap 36 he retired on Segrave Straight with a faulty gearbox. A little later, on lap 41, Cuth Harrison's ERA, which had briefly worked its way up to a splendid fifth place (when Bira stopped for fuel) and had steadily held sixth ahead of de Graffenried, Bolster, Hampshire and Walker (no mean achievement) retired with a broken valve.

Of the British survivors, Bob Gerard continued to impress, helped by his ability to extract between 7,000 and 7,500 rpm from his engine (whereas most ERAs were limited to 6,500). He was driving, wrote one admirer, 'with tremendous accuracy, barely once skidding a turn, but being held back by his control'. By lap 36 he had overtaken Rosier and Bira (whose brake linings were now badly worn) and only Villoresi and Ascari were in front of

him. On lap 39 he finally stopped for fuel. The precision of his pit crew was in such marked contrast to the others it reminded one observer of the pre-war Mercedes Grand Prix team. Typical of their attention to detail was the use of funnels with the petrol churns and the protection given to Gerard's back during the refuelling process. Dennis Poore, a rich business entrepreneur and racing driver who would shortly put up the money for the creation of *Autosport*, had been noticeably active in Gerard's pit, stopwatch in hand, leading earnest calculations like the quantity of new fuel needed (30 gallons). Gerard's re-entry to the race after this calm and efficient forty-eight-second stop drew tremendous applause from the grandstands. But Rosier was once more ahead of him…

* * *

Guy Griffiths, standing at the intersection, was struck by just how much the leaders were now spaced out. Villoresi had long disappeared before Ascari arrived, and the leading Maserati was now a full three minutes in front of Rosier, who, despite not having to stop for fuel, would soon be lapped. Gerard, in fourth, was slowly closing down the considerable gap to Rosier and was well ahead of the ailing Bira.

But Guy Griffiths was still excited. Partly, of course, that was the exhilaration of ignoring the warnings that 'motor racing is dangerous' and standing by the side of the track as cars braked hard from between 140 mph and 150 mph. But there was something more than that. Something to do with the purity of line of a thoroughbred racing car (the ERAs and Maseratis were the Anna Neagles and Anna Magnanis of the racetrack, exuding glamour from every pore) and something to do with atmosphere (the potency, in particular, of that all-pervasive aroma of burnt racing oil). Guy had been hooked by fast cars early, ever since he and Peter Whitehead communed endlessly at school about the heroes of Brooklands. There had been a tradition there that when the bishop came for confirmation services, he would present candidates with Bibles previously bought and wrapped by the pupils' parents. Guy had persuaded his parents to wrap up Sammy Davis's *Motor Racing*.

* * *

The main interest in the race had become the midfield battle between the troubled Maserati of de Graffenried and the well-matched ERAs of Hampshire, Walker, Bolster and Nixon. George Nixon was doing tremendously well to keep these much more experienced drivers in sight. But Peter 'Skid' Walker, who normally would have been disappointed to be so far back, was being hampered by weak brakes and would eventually drop out altogether with engine trouble.

John Bolster, having recovered from the shock of Geoff Ansell's accident, was again having a good time. It was a real thrill to have become (at least for one afternoon) a Grand Prix star watched by thousands of people in Britain's big race and it brought out all his

Gigi Villoresi lines up Segrave Corner. The first of the two hangars down Hangar Straight looms large to his left. (*Guy Griffiths Collection*)

Raymond Mays at the central intersection shortly before retiring from the race. (*Guy Griffiths Collection*)

histrionic tendencies. During his pitstop at around half distance he had yelled at the top of his voice for more water – there had been signs of overheating – and then he had dramatically cowered down in his seat as a mackintosh was thrown over him in case of refuelling error. Under the mackintosh, he eagerly cleaned his goggles and started priming the hand pump, so that as soon as the tank filler was shut, the fuel would at once be delivered to the carburettor. And as the mackintosh was swept away from him, he leapt back at the wheel, pointing forwards with an outstretched arm in the direction of Woodcote and encouraging the mechanics to strain every sinew on the push-start. He was so taken with the drama of it all, so overwhelmed by his apparent power to draw ecstatic applause from the grandstands, that he swerved back into the race oblivious of cars pounding up the pits straight, only a few feet away, 'getting short of shock absorbers and brakes and becoming a bit wild in consequence'. It was always a strange experience going out from the pits mid-race. For just a few seconds everyone seemed to be going so crazily fast. And then 'it all seemed right and natural again'. He was soon back in the midfield scrap.

* * *

Geoff Richardson in his Riley-ERA special at Club. (*Guy Griffiths Collection*)

R.A.C. GRAND PRIX.
RACE LEADERS AT 42 LAPS

	1ST	2ND	3RD	4TH	5TH
NUMBER	18	11	3	16	19

Lap 42. Team manager Enrico Platé pours in water
as de Graffenried looks underneath his Maserati.
The scoreboard tells the grandstand spectators that
Villoresi leads from Ascari, Rosier, Gerard and Bira.
(*Guy Griffiths Collection*)

Alan Hess was not best pleased. The BBC had allocated him one final quarter-of-an-hour for what listeners had been promised would be a description of the finish. Unfortunately, whoever had calculated the end of the race had seriously got his arithmetic wrong, and by the time the race ended the Band of the Coldstream Guards would be well into their half-hour programme. All he could do, therefore, was to cover the latest situation – Gerard had just over taken Rosier for third place; Ascari was currently thirty seconds behind Villoresi – and encourage listeners to tune in to *Sports Report* later that evening, when he would be giving a short summary.

* * *

The spectators in the grandstand opposite the pits had had the best of things, for the pits held the major excitement in the second half of the race. The George Bainbridge/Bob Ansell Maserati paid several visits with its incurable oil leak, until the offending car was finally flagged off the course. Another reserve driver, Philip Fotheringham-Parker (a forty-one-year-old who had once gone over the Brooklands banking and landed miraculously in a tree) had taken over David Hampshire's ERA. Soon afterwards he returned in the stuttering car to remove bits of marker barrel from the ERA's front suspension. With Hampshire back at the wheel, it started going decently again, overtaking Salvadori and the stricken de Graffenried and rising to seventh.

De Graffenried, who was loving the slippery circuit and applying armfuls of opposite lock at each corner, had stopped several times to take on water, with clouds of steam dramatically enveloping the pit each time, but the biggest excitement came with the leading Maseratis' final stops for fuel and oil. First Villoresi, lap 50, for just twenty-five seconds. Then, lap 52, Ascari, for thirty-five seconds.

* * *

Gigi was letting Alberto draw closer. There was so much oil on the track. His wheels were constantly picking it up and flinging it at his face and goggles; he himself felt caked in it, but he was not going to throw the race away at this late stage. He was not letting the loss of his rev counter bother him either, nor had the fact that when it shook itself free from the dashboard it unluckily chose to lodge under his clutch, rendering that pedal

Above: George Bainbridge in Bob Ansell's damaged Maserati. (*Guy Griffiths Collection*)

Opposite: George Nixon presses relentlessly on in ERA R2A. (*Guy Griffiths Collection*)

useless. The one-minute gap to Alberto immediately after the pitstops had come down by a half. But Gigi had no intention of being generous and giving Alberto the race. Only last May at Monaco, when Alberto had retired with a broken oil pump, he had stopped to let him take over his own car. But generosity could only go so far! Alberto had many years ahead of him. He would win here in the future. Gigi had thirty seconds in hand with just five laps left and that should be enough. The race was surely his now…

* * *

Bira was bored. He had been going round and round this featureless circuit for longer than he cared to think about. Sheer

Below: Peter Walker struggles on through his problems in Peter Whitehead's elderly ERA.

Opposite: Toulo de Graffenried drives off through the Ambrosiana pits. Bertocchi (far right) suggests caution. (*Guy Griffiths Collection*)

purgatory. And life was not meant to be purgatory, it was meant to be a series of pleasurable adventures. The evenings had been all right. He had enjoyed himself away from the aerodrome, but the aerodrome was intolerable, lacking in every basic amenity!

Bira was cross. He was in fifth place, just as he had been for the last umpteen laps, over six minutes behind Gigi. He had been lapped twice, and they were meant to be in identical cars, and his the newer! Chula had really failed him with this last gift. He'd been fooled by the Italians, who delivered a machine with a whole series of inbuilt faults, from the inferior superchargers to the derisory brakes. He had been having to slow on the gears for the last thirty laps – ridiculous! And he was meant to be driving it this coming weekend at Montlhéry. Well, that would depend on Stan Holgate sorting out at least some of its problems.

Bira was disgusted. It was all right for Gigi and his friend Alberto to be out in front. They were both as quick as he was. But Bob Gerard third in an old ERA? That was ridiculous! And Louis Rosier fourth in his Talbot? He was a lovely person and a brave one, too, but hardly rapier quick. Yet Rosier, despite going much slower than usual, had ended up well ahead of him! And here he was, in his new toy, which Chula had assured him would be really fast, trying to keep ahead of that bumptious John Bolster in Remus, a car that he himself had owned before the war.

Bira was thoughtful. Perhaps if this Maserati couldn't be sorted he would be better off doing a deal with Enzo Ferrari? That new Ferrari 125 that he had driven last month in Torino might handle like a pig but the engine certainly had power. He had enjoyed meeting Ferrari at Modena before the race. He and Ceril had a good time there. Ferrari's son Dino had loved the

Miles Gemini and all the various gadgets he'd installed in it. The lunch at the *Boninsegna* had been very amicable. Ferrari was clearly interested in him. There'd be a 125 available to him at Barcelona at the end of the month. He'd definitely take that up. But Ferrari, for all his interest, seemed to have some reservations.

Above: Petrol is poured into Bob Gerard's ERA via a funnel. (*Guy Griffiths Collection*)

Opposite: Bob Gerard is push-started after his second and last pitstop. (*Guy Griffiths Collection*)

That question about whether or not he'd put a day of testing above a day's gliding had suggested some reservations. And his truthful answer had seemed to pain Ferrari.

Bira was relieved. Five laps to go! And later on this evening, away from this extraordinary wilderness, the day could begin in earnest...

* * *

Rodney Walkerley, sitting in his hut in the potato field, had enjoyed himself hugely. As a sociable motoring journalist, talking came naturally to him. To have well over 100,000 to talk to was a particular privilege, and the three hours in the cramped box had been as nothing. And now, as the race reached its climax, here was de Graffenried coming into sight yet again at Abbey, a long way behind the leaders, but still all arms and elbows, luxuriating in the oily surface.

This time, however, to his surprise, de Graffenried seemed to have misjudged things, entering Abbey too fast and completely losing the car as he tried to make the apex of the left-hander, spinning at considerable speed across the track, hitting some straw bales with a tremendous thump and then skidding some 50 yards into the potato field, collecting, as he did so, some of the wiring connected to the PA system. The captured wiring went round and round de Graffenried's Maserati, as the car spewed earth and potatoes from its wheels, trying to regain traction, and Walkerley found himself pulled out of his seat, the microphone falling from his hands. Worse might have followed had the furious Swiss Baron not stopped his efforts at extracting the Maserati from the field. As de Graffenried stalked away from his car, Walkerley resettled at the microphone. Villoresi must be starting his last lap...

* * *

Gigi, taking Woodcote for the sixty-fifth and last time, treated it with care, partly because he knew he was at least twenty seconds ahead of Alberto and partly because the crowd had moved in front of the rope barrier and was now lining the edge of the track. It was the same all the way down the straight to Copse, a blur of arms waving and programmes quivering in the air. His heart went out to them. He couldn't hear a thing – he was temporarily deaf – and he could hardly see them – too much oil on his goggles – but they were cheering him to the echo, he was sure of it, cheering him, Luigi Villoresi, who only three years earlier had been imprisoned in this very country after his capture in the African desert. That, of course, would always be his secret. They knew only that he, Luigi, was the leading driver of Maserati. But even that would have been enough three years ago to have ostracised him here. They were cheering the red of Italy. They were cheering the return of Grand Prix racing to Britain. And they were cheering him, Luigi Villoresi, even though their own British heroes had long since been vanquished!

It was good to have the peace of the runway leading to the intersection, to gather up his thoughts. He was driving fast – 150 mph. He wanted to win. He loved Alberto like only one brother can love another, but he still wanted to win! Not so much for himself. For Emilio, perhaps, the brother who perished at Monza and never lived to visit Britain. For his mother, most certainly, who so often would be at the end of the Mille Miglia or the Targa Florio, waiting to embrace him, to congratulate him for whatever honours he may have won, and for emerging from another race without giving her cause for further grief. Yes, this race was for his mother.

An oil-spattered Alberto Ascari smoothly enters Segrave. (*Guy Griffiths Collection*)

The crowds were waving again as he approached the right-hander at Maggot's. Strangely, he wanted to win the race for them, too, for all those waving and showing him admiration and affection. It was such therapy. Only Alberto knew how much, deep down, he had dreaded this expedition. Of course, he had to make it. He had known that from the moment *il gentiluomo* Howe had first broached it. He had friends in England, friends who wanted to forget the war as much as he did, friends who saw the bigger picture. He was travelling flat out down Hangar Straight. There was no chance of Alberto catching him now – he was out in front alone, with no one in his mirrors.

Rounding Stowe, strangely empty of people, he headed up the runway to the intersection. He hardly noticed that he had no clutch and no rev counter. He was driving automatically, at one with the machinery, nursing it with a tenderness belied by all the noise. This was the corner coming up where he had overcooked things and gone through the oil drums. Not this time! He was soon rattling down to Club. He could barely hear the engine, loud though it was howling! His gear changes were pure intuition as he slowed for the tight right-hander that would lead him past Enclosure A. The crowd had come nearer. They, too, were standing by the side of the road, all the way up to Abbey, on his left, cheering and waving, seemingly desperate to share in his victory. Hats, too, were being raised in good old English fashion. *Grazie a Dio!*

* * *

Rodney Walkerley, none the worse for the contretemps with de Graffenried and steadying himself with a cigarette, was his usual calm and matter-of-fact self as he described the final scene from the hut in the potato field:

There's Colonel Barnes! He now has the chequered flag. He's waiting to flag Villoresi as he comes round Abbey Curve. I think you'll admit, ladies and gentlemen, it's been a magnificent race. Here's the flag up! And here's Villoresi, roaring up to the line, and he's past it and slowing down, having won the Grand Prix!

Exiting Abbey, Gigi had briefly sighted a red Maserati to his right that had to be Toulo's. Briefly, too, he had sighted Alberto, just taking the left-hander at the intersection. So he had been able to relax and enjoy the gentle climb to the footbridge, slowing down well before he reached the line. There was his number, 18, raised aloft, as the chequered flag was waved! The line of pits, all along on his right, was packed with people overflowing onto the track, and the road in front of him was being swallowed up by an incoming tide of massed humanity! He stopped as close as he could get to his pits. There was Bertocchi, thrusting an opened bottle of ginger beer into his hands, happy as could be! Gigi gulped and smiled, gulped more and waved, as all around the dirty Maserati came the jubilant, swelling crowd. Gigi had won *their* Grand Prix! Italian red had vanquished British green! And yet – *Grazie a Dio* – such enthusiasm! Such a demonstration of affection!

'The drivers and the cars at the pits,' wrote one reporter, 'went down under a sea of living flesh.' Another reckoned the crowd sweeping onto the track was of several thousands: 'They could not be kept back and officials good-humouredly accepted the inevitable, as they crushed and crowded into the centre of enthusiasm with newsreel vehicles towering above them.'

Two triumphant Maseratis. In the melée, Guy would seem to have been unable to select the right exposure for his photograph, but he has, nonetheless, captured an important moment in British motor racing history. (*Guy Griffiths Collection*)

A laurel wreath from Lady Howe. (*Guy Griffiths Collection*)

Villoresi and Ascari celebrate with bottles of ginger beer provided by Bertocchi. Count Johnny **Lurani** joins in the celebration. (*Guy Griffiths Collection*)

CHAPTER 14

There was no question of a lap of honour. The remaining nine finishers, warned by some vigorous flag waving, slowed down and somehow all managed to make their way to the pits. Ascari had crossed the line fourteen seconds adrift of Villoresi and drawn up behind him. The 'delighted, dirty and deaf' John Bolster had to be helped out of his car, having burnt his foot against the gearbox.

The official prize-giving, planned to take place in front of the start-line grandstand half an hour after the end of the race, was clearly no longer possible. Countess Howe was escorted by Wilfrid Andrews through the crowds to the front of the Ambrosiana pits, where she put large laurel wreaths round the necks of the two Italians. A quick handshake from Wilfrid Andrews followed and the ceremony, such as it was, was over. Everyone made for the temporary refuge of the paddock area. Gigi and Alberto found themselves besieged by well-wishers, the situation becoming so impossible that they eventually fled to the Lancia Aprilia and made an inglorious escape from the circuit, bouncing over, and bumping through, various agricultural obstacles. They so damaged the car that it was taken later that evening to Bill Grose's Northampton garage for repairs.

* * *

The attempt of 130,000 spectators to leave the circuit began almost immediately and the track, from Abbey to Copse, was soon occupied by lines of cars and coaches, four or five abreast, inching their way towards the one exit from opposite directions.

Various tales of woe were later published in *The Motor*: 'I noticed only three RAC Scouts on leaving,' wrote one grumbler, 'and there were a number of quite disinterested policemen and other officials watching the maelstrom without helping to ease things at all. I know of one coach which did not get away until 10.45 p.m. For myself, I must have been one of the lucky ones. I managed to get out in two and a half hours.' 'My wife attended, in a bus run by a local motor club,' wrote another, 'and boarded this at 5.20 for the return journey. At 8.45, the time they were due home, the bus was still on the aerodrome, and she eventually arrived at midnight. A good day was completely ruined.'

As darkness fell at the aerodrome, the perimeter road became 'a vast fairyland of thousands of lights of vehicles awaiting their turn to hit the highway'. It was around 10.00 p.m. when the 30,000 vehicles eventually escaped. John Bolster, towing away his borrowed caravan, was among the more dynamic of leavers: 'The car parks were still jammed hours after the race, so we simply engaged four-wheel drive on the Jeep and drove across meadows, ditches, hedges and woods ... we had to get to a pub somehow!'

Reporters at nearby towns described unprecedented sights. 'The procession of lighted cars down Stowe Avenue,' declared the *Buckingham Advertiser*, 'had something of the stately beauty of a torch-lit procession. Crowds turned out to watch the passage of the lighted cars through Buckingham.' Brackley was similarly en fête. 'The Market Square in the evening could not accommodate a perambulator.'

* * *

Geoffrey Samuelson was soon supervising the allocation of prize money to the top ten cars. To Villoresi: £500. To Ascari: £300. To Gerard: £200. He had kept to himself the suspicion that it had not been the greatest of races, with only three cars on the same lap at the end of the three hours twenty minutes of racing, and Gerard, in third place, over two minutes behind Ascari and Villoresi. Nor did he think it tactful to raise with Lord Howe the fact that, for the last twenty-seven laps – well over a third of the race – the same six cars had been going round in exactly the same order. Louis Rosier (£100) in fourth place was one lap and over four and a half minutes behind Villoresi; and Prince Bira (£75) and John Bolster (£50) in fifth and sixth were two laps down. Final payments were made to David Hampshire (£40) in seventh, all of five laps down; Roy Salvadori (£30) and Toulo de Graffenried (£25) in eighth and ninth, six laps down. George Nixon, who ended up seven laps down, received the last prize (£20).

* * *

Two days after the race, on the evening of Monday 4 October, the BRDC held a dinner in London to honour the foreign drivers. The Piccadilly Hotel, newly opened by a friend of Lord Howe's at No. 96 Piccadilly, provided the venue for 140 members and their guests, who 'assembled in a highly festive mood and fêted the successful and consoled the unfortunate'. Villoresi was the last guest to arrive. He explained smilingly that he'd given his evening dress trousers to a hotel chambermaid asking for them to be carefully pressed, instead of which they had been completely mislaid.

Over the post-dinner toasts, Howe took the opportunity of announcing that he was in touch with the FIA with a view to another RAC Grand Prix at Silverstone, this time with the title of 'British', to take place next June. Bob Gerard received the ovation of the evening and 'was even forced to say a few words'. Louis Chiron, who needed less persuasion, made a slightly provocative speech, remarking ruefully that 'these days one had to go to Italy to buy racing cars' and 'what a pity it was that the British didn't get down to the job on a large scale'. Ignoring loud interruptions of 'Wait for the BRM!', Chiron turned to a subject close to his heart. It was a pity, too, he said, that 'at this Grand Prix there had not been enough give'! He'd just been invited to appear on the BBC Television service later in the week and, he assured everyone, he was certainly going to mention that there had not been enough give! Lord Howe, refusing to rise to Chiron's cheerful jibes, replied with dignity that in most people's view the starting money had been more than generous.

Gigi gave a little speech in English, 'which was much applauded, perhaps because they had understood little of what I said!' Alberto followed in French, with asides in Italian to Gigi and Ramponi asking, 'How do you say that in French?' Both Italians charmed their English hosts. The wine flowed all evening and such was the conviviality that when the comedian Jimmy Edwards (of the popular radio series *Take It From Here!*) led the post-dinner entertainment, he received a distinctly raucous reception.

CHAPTER 15

It would be many months more before the RAC could complete the full balance sheet, which would reveal a large investment of £18,991 5s 7d in putting on the meeting and an overall loss of over £3,000. In the early weeks after the race, Geoffrey Samuelson's desk was littered with reports reviewing race day. Overall takings at the gate had amounted to £6,920 5s 0d and programme sales £1,114 8s 3d. But clearly the collecting of admission money had left much to be desired. 'I enclose 30s to pay for my most enjoyable day last Saturday at Silverstone,' wrote one spectator to him. 'Your attendants were far too busy to worry about taking money off me when I arrived!' Mr Whetstone of the RAC's Road Patrols Department reported that the ticket-selling staff had been 'sorely tried', the collection of admission fees continuing throughout the day, 'even after the conclusion of racing when vehicles were moving out'. Mr Darling, meanwhile, from the Associate Accounts Dept., who had spent much of the day in the Westminster Bank security van collecting up the takings, reported that the vehicle had been 'rather too big for manoeuvring in the lanes of the car parks and travelling over meadowland'. At 7.00 p.m. they were still making collections from catering outlets and programme sellers.

Whetstone was full of helpful ideas. It was crystal clear, he wrote, that for future events the first essential was additional entrance roads that would feed traffic into the rear of the enclosures and make it unnecessary to use the perimeter track. Jimmy Brown fully concurred: 'More damage was done to track equipment by spectators' cars after the racing than by the actual racing cars. Cars were allowed to drive round the circuit of their own free will and more severe damage to life and limb could have been done, as well as damage to track and equipment.'

There was a need, continued Whetstone, for a larger grandstand capacity, but the practice of allowing spectators in on the practice days should be stopped: 'Stewards should be on duty to keep stands clear and thus preserve the numbering. On 1 October persons were seen leaving the Stands with the still wet number labels adhering to their shoes.' There should be a greater police presence, and 'it should be impressed on Police that they are there to do a job of work and not to witness a day's motor racing'. Marshals likewise came in for criticism: 'Marshals should line boundary fences and hedges to prevent irregular entry of pedestrians. They also must realise that if they volunteer for a day's duty they are expected to carry out their obligations even to the extent of seeing nothing at all of the racing. *The Autocar*'s Sammy Davis agreed: 'Far too many of them formed crowds to watch the race and took French leave from their jobs.'

Three weeks after the race, Jimmy Brown and Col. Barnes attended a meeting convened by the Air Ministry's Inspector of Works to examine the post-race condition of the runways and perimeter road under the guidance of an emeritus Professor of Highway Engineering from Imperial College, London. Professor Clements declared that no damage had been caused and the only complaint from the Air Ministry was the large amount of oil that had been dropped.

Brown himself, whose temporary job as track manager had already been put on a permanent basis, had any number of points to make to the RAC. It would be important to take over several Air Ministry buildings another time, and of those he had in mind, near the guardhouse, one was currently being used by Rootes without permission. Then there was the vexed question of boundary fences. Did this rest, he asked, with the Air Ministry, the RAC or jointly with the current tenants (Rootes Group and the Bucks Agricultural Executive Committee)?

He had surveyed the possibility of entrance from the Whittlebury side of the aerodrome with Northampton's Town and Planning Office, but the sheer length of the road made entrance via Mr Graham's farm impractical. Other routes under review posed legal difficulties, and he urged the creation of further entrances on the Dadford lane. Brown also made useful comments on the track layout. He had no criticism of the confrontational nature of the central intersection, but felt some 'artificial features' might be put in to make the course more interesting. 'Suggest early decision so that experiments can be carried out and work put in hand.'

Rodney Walkerley aired in *The Motor* the idea that the entire length of the main runway might be used, from Copse right down to Stowe, to avoid the excessively slow corners at Seaman and Segrave, which 'would raise the lap speeds greatly, but more or less halve the lap distance.' If the present track layout were to continue, he wrote, grandstands should be put up at Segrave and Seaman corners and ramps created in all spectator enclosures. 'A raised platform for the prize presentation would also be helpful.'

By the end of December, the RAC had paid its subscription of £18 to the FIA, the first step in making the Grand Prix of 1949 fully 'British'.

CHAPTER 16

The International Grand Prix of 1948 was to be the only Race of the runways. That December the RAC announced that a new layout, using just the perimeter road, had been tested by Bob Gerard and would be the format for 1949. Soon there were other 'sensational revelations': the circuit would be available for hire for private testing and clubs promoting their own meetings; improved spectator facilities would include new grandstands; and, in addition to the RAC's Grand Prix, the BRDC would be promoting an annual International Trophy meeting for Grand Prix cars, sponsored by the *Daily Express*.

* * *

Not all the participants of the Race of the Runways were to witness Silverstone's steady development. Geoffrey Ansell, who had appeared to have made a full recovery from his big crash at Maggot's and had raced, like his cousin Bob, for a further year before retiring, died suddenly in January 1951, aged only thirty-one. By 1951, moreover, three of the 500 drivers, Chris Smith, Joe Fry and 'Curly' Dryden, had been killed, and in 1952 the whole nation felt a deep sense of loss when John Cobb's attempt on the World Water Speed Record ended in tragedy at Loch Ness. Cobb had regularly returned to Silverstone as a steward at the big meetings and had rediscovered personal happiness in a second marriage. Newsreels showed Lord Howe, his friend and fellow Old Etonian, among the mourners at the funeral at Esher. In 1953, Bobby Baird, the Irishman whose Emeryson proved so recalcitrant in the two Grand Prix practice sessions, was killed and the following year Enrico Platé, de Graffenried's flamboyant team manager, was mown down by a car spinning into the pits at a race in South America. Another 500 driver, Ken Wharton, after a late blossoming career, lost his life in a Ferrari in 1957.

Louis Rosier's good luck also eventually deserted him. A much quicker driver than his performance at Silverstone had suggested, he won several Grands Prix afterwards as well as Le Mans and, under his own Ecurie Rosier banner, he also ran other drivers (Louis Chiron among them) right up to his death at Montlhéry in 1956. Duncan Hamilton, competing in the same sports car race, was following Rosier as he lost control entering a high-speed bend. Rosier's Ferrari overturned and bounced right over Hamilton, the Ferrari's bonnet brushing his helmet. The quiet, chain-smoking hero of the French Resistance died in hospital several days later, aged fifty. 'As I stood by his grave after the funeral service was over,' wrote Hamilton, 'I wondered whether the thrill and excitement of the race was worthwhile when it so often ended like this … Louis was a very great friend and a great sportsman.' A racetrack at Clermont Ferrand (that he himself had suggested) was later opened as the *Circuit de Charade Louis Rosier.*

Leslie Johnson outlived Rosier by three years. He continued trying to develop the E-type ERA, but enjoyed greater success in long-distance sports car races like the Mille Miglia, Le Mans and Spa. Ill-health continued to dog him, and a heart attack in 1952 ended the F-type ERA project and led to the sale of the ERA company. He retired from motor sport after another heart attack, while competing in the 1954 Monte Carlo Rally, and acquired a Gloucestershire farm where he had three houses built: one for himself and his wife (the widow of a teammate killed at Le Mans), one for his farm manager and one for his accountant. He died five years later, aged forty-six. His stepson remembered him as 'very warm, very kind and great fun'.

* * *

Franco Comotti, the former wartime spy, died in his native Bergamo in 1963 aged fifty-six. After returning to Italy, he attracted occasional drives in older machinery in F1 and F2 for a few years. He prospered in business, working for BP around the Mediterranean. Just before his death he helped found the *Club International des Anciens Pilotes de Grand Prix F1.*

The career of his contemporary, Reg Parnell, by contrast, flourished for another nine years. His Ambrosiana links remained strong in the immediate aftermath of the Race of the

Right and opposite: Duncan Hamilton's Maserati 6CM, Silverstone 2013. (*D. Hyslop*)

Runways, and the Scuderia entered his Maserati (along with those of Villoresi and Fred Ashmore) at the RAC's next Grand Prix. Equipped at last with the latest superchargers and brakes, Parnell stayed with the Scuderia, consolidating his position as Britain's leading international driver. Though in 1951, amid some acrimony, his Maserati was taken back by Ambrosiana's Count Lurani, Parnell remained highly competitive in both sports cars and single-seaters, achieving twenty-one major victories, many in Aston Martins and Ferraris. After retirement he increased his farming activities and went into team management, including the Le Mans-winning Aston Martins. The very talented and popular Parnell was running his own Formula 1 team for Mike Hailwood and Chris Amon at the time of his sudden death in January 1964.

Six months later, in July 1964, the British Racing Drivers' Club lost its long-time president with the death of the eighty-year-old Lord Howe. He had lived long enough to steer the circuit through two important changes. In 1952, the BRDC took over the Air Ministry lease from the RAC, at the same time moving the start-line, pits and paddock to just beyond Woodcote. And in 1960 protracted negotiations began that led to the BRDC's purchase of the circuit, along with the acquisition of the company that had been running the farm. Howe died shortly after the opening of the new, elevated pits.

Wilfrid Andrews, whose support Howe had so importantly engaged in 1948, remained the RAC's Chairman right up to 1972, when, at the age of eighty, he retired to a suite at the club's country house, Woodcote Park, where he remained influential as 'Chairman d'honneur'. In the 1960s, Andrews had become the first British president of motor sport's international governing body, the *Fédération Internationale de l'Automobile*. Ever the autocrat, he insisted on proceedings being conducted in English rather than French and moved most of the meetings from the Paris headquarters to London.

* * *

Above and opposite: Raymond Mays' ERA, Silverstone 2013. (*D. Hyslop*)

Louis Chiron raced on with Ecurie France, winning the French Grand Prix of 1949 in the Lago-Talbot. Though Paul Vallée (who died in 1957, aged fifty-two) disbanded his team at the end of that year to concentrate on manufacturing scooters, Chiron found further backing, winning the Monte Carlo Rally in 1954 and entering his last Grand Prix in 1958 at the age of fifty-eight. After a career spanning thirty-five years, he became a well-known (and flamboyantly autocratic) *Commissaire Général* at the Grand Prix in his hometown, Monaco. The bronze bust on the memorial erected to him down by the harbour (after his death, aged seventy-nine, in 1979) shows Chiron looking his dapper best, goggles dangling underneath a smart cravat. In 1997, the first part of the swimming pool complex at Monaco was named 'Louis Chiron'.

Raymond Mays died a few months after Chiron, in January 1980, aged eighty, his struggles with the BRM already part of motor racing history. Though Reg Parnell won two short races in the BRM at Goodwood shortly after the terrible embarrassment of 1950 (the abject demise of the much-heralded car on the starting-grid at Silverstone), it was not until the end of the decade that the BRM finally won a Grand Prix, by which time Mays and Berthon had given way to Tony Rudd. Such disappointments might have destroyed a lesser man, but Mays maintained a broad view of life. He never lost, for example, his love of the theatre, and even at the height of the problems he was able to find solace in a first night, particularly delighting in Ivor Novello's Ruritanian musical of 1949 at Drury Lane, *King's Rhapsody*, and the performance of Phyllis Dare, whom he had admired since boyhood. His garage at Bourne prospered, too, as a Ford dealership, and for several years the Mays name

was used for tuning equipment, including a special cylinder head designed by Peter Berthon. Mays was awarded the CBE in 1978, six years after the death of his mother, Annie. In his will, he left over 120 silver cups to various friends. He had given many more away in his lifetime, and his mother usually selected one of her son's cups when she needed a wedding present.

Cuth Harrison raced on for three more seasons in his well-prepared but outdated equipment. At forty-four, he decided

Above and opposite: Bolster's ex-Bira ERA Remus, back in Siamese colours, Silverstone 2013. (*D. Hyslop*)

to devote himself more fully to his garage business and enjoy himself at weekends with a trials car. He duly became RAC Trials Champion in 1952 and the T. C. Harrison Ford dealership, later taken over by his sons and grandsons, still celebrates his name throughout the Midlands. He died in 1981.

Philippe Étancelin won the Paris Grand Prix and achieved several second places with his Lago-Talbot in 1949. He only finally retired in 1953, at the age of fifty-six, having just come third at Rouen. He died in his native Normandy in 1981 and is commemorated by the Rue Philippe Étancelin in Saint-Gaudens, the organising town of the Comminges Grand Prix, which he had won back in 1929 and 1931.

Peter Walker had a troubled later life after some distinguished drives for the Jaguar works team (including a Le Mans victory) and the difficult sixteen-cylinder BRM. 'Peter was a great charmer,' remembered fellow Aston Martin driver, Jack Fairman.

Above and below right: Gianfranco Comotti's Talbot, photographed in 2004 in the USA at around the time it was auctioned for half a million dollars. It still has its original upholstery. (*Chris Kelley/Fantasy Junction*)

Opposite: Earl Howe's Buckinghamshire home, Penn House.

Inset: In the 1930s, Earl Howe introduced banked corners into the southern approach to his house, creating a stimulating challenge of 2 miles with more than a hint of the Nürburgring.

'He always had a fantastic sense of humour – he could make anyone laugh.' He invented a novel way of making butter, for example, tying a churn of cream to a rear wheel of his Jaguar and driving it up and down his farm till the contents thickened. But his demons were never far away. 'He would have been a better driver,' said Fairman, 'if he'd laid off the drink a bit, but when he was in the right mood, he was undoubtedly the fastest driver of his day, even quicker than Stirling.' The collapse of his marriage was followed by a bad crash at Le Mans in 1956 and retirement, aged forty-three, when he threw away everything connected with his glamorous past. A farming business with a new partner failed, as did a project to design a novel cattle grid. His last years were tragically dark. He died in 1984 aged seventy-two.

In May 1949, at the second RAC Grand Prix, John Bolster's racing career received a major setback with a terrible crash at Stowe Corner, when Remus skidded on oil, slid into a hay bale, overturned and ejected Bolster with such ferocity that he lost most of his clothing as he slid down the road. 'It also somersaulted end over end, during which caper it caught up with me again and damaged the few parts of me that were in one piece up till then.' As he lay on the side of the track, in agony but still conscious, the ambulance went to the wrong corner. There was no doctor on hand to administer painkillers. 'Even in my desperate position I heard the crowd boo the ambulance when it at last arrived.' Injuries included a broken neck and partial paralysis, but in time Bolster made a complete recovery. In his early forties, he found new diversions from farming as a motor racing commentator (he was much-parodied for his deerstalker and other eccentricities) and as technical editor of the newly-launched *Autosport*. Heart trouble slowed him

down, but he was lucky that his young third wife, Rosemary, was happy to turn the handle of his beloved Silver Ghost. He died in the winter of 1984, aged seventy-three, leaving £20 in his will for more fuel for the church's boiler to keep everyone warm at his funeral.

Prince Bira's Maserati brought him considerable success in 1949 when he raced with de Graffenried in Enrico Platé's team and, but for a disappointing crash, would have won Silverstone's second Grand Prix. Thereafter Bira struggled to acquire the cars to do justice to his natural flair, until the purchase in 1954 of a 250F Maserati brought final victories at the *Grand Prix des Frontières* at Chimay and the New Zealand Grand Prix. He retired in 1955.

In his later life, the multi-talented prince badly missed the steadying influences of his cousin, Chula, and first love, Ceril. Money, like wives and mistresses, came and went; fortunes, to be gained through high finance, car sales and an airfreight company, proved elusive. He bravely flew from London to Bangkok in his Miles Gemini and wrote a book about it; he represented Thailand in sailing at four different Olympic Games (between 1956 and 1972); he skied with distinction; he flew for Thai Airlines; he flirted with supernatural help from a dead Buddhist saint; he began an autobiography; he changed his name to Mr Osca; and enlivened the lives of all with whom he came into contact. Having flirted with death for much of his life, he met

Opposite: Bira's car in the paddock after it crashed out of the 1949 Grand Prix. Smith and Brenda Churchill examine the damage with a friend. (*Graham Churchill*)

it from a heart attack on the platform of a London tube station (Baron's Court) in 1985, aged seventy-one.

If Bira lacked focus, not so Jimmy Brown, who became a Silverstone legend, serving the circuit for forty years till his death in 1988. Since Segrave and Seaman ceased to be commemorated with the abolition of their corners and straights in 1949, it had not been Silverstone's way to celebrate great figures of the past (not even the BRDC's long-serving president, Earl Howe), but Jimmy proved the single exception when the Jimmy Brown Centre was opened.

Gordon Watson competed with an Alta for four more seasons after 1948, purchasing a new Formula 2 model in 1950 from the company's owner-designer, Geoffrey Taylor, whose premises in Kingston were conveniently within reach. A typical gentleman driver who raced for the sheer fun of it, Gordon happened to get married on the second anniversary of the Race of the Runways and celebrated by driving in his wedding clothes, top hat and all, through Egham High Street to his bride's home in Englefield Green in his rorty Alta. When racing at Silverstone they would often stay at the Weston Manor Hotel, and Gordon's widow, Marjorie, has memories of joyful times there, with young drivers like Mike Hawthorn (a neighbour and close friend) to the fore

Right: Mays and Parnell in the Jersey pits, 1949. (*John Pearson*)

Opposite: Spectator protection still looking fairly minimal as Gordon Watson exits Woodcote, International Trophy, 1950. (*Marjorie Watson*)

in splendid jollities. Gordon regretfully retired from racing at thirty-three, no longer feeling that the rising costs of staying at the top level of the sport were justifiable. A lifelong member of the BRDC, he would often visit Silverstone, sometimes in a vintage Alvis or Bentley, and he successfully satisfied his passion for exotic cars and all things mechanical right up to his death in 1989, just before his seventieth birthday.

* * *

David Hampshire came fourth in the RAC's 1949 Grand Prix, drove an Ambrosiana Maserati with his friend Reg Parnell in 1950, and later diversified into international sports cars and historic racing. Having retired from the family's pharmaceutical business in his late fifties, he moved to Mallorca and on to Monaco before returning to a Derbyshire village, where he died in 1990, aged seventy-two.

Bob Gerard, who died the same year, four years older, had done even better in 1949, finishing a magnificent second at the Silverstone Grand Prix. He went on to further successes in Cooper-Bristols and was a regular competitor in the British Grand Prix up to 1957. After retiring four years later, he devoted much time to Bob Gerard Racing, helping foster as a team manager the careers of many notable drivers until the early 1980s, while continuing to run the family garage business, which held the Leicestershire Honda franchise. One of the corners at Mallory Park was named 'Gerard's' in his honour.

George Nixon, who also died in 1990, had found his old ERA woefully outclassed in the 1949 Grand Prix and so, faced with the need to buy new equipment, he spent some time out of racing building up his Staffordshire garage businesses. By 1954, his flourishing Ford dealerships had put him in a position to enjoy

six years' more fun, first with sports-racing cars and finally with a couple of Formula 1 and 2 single-seater Coopers. His daughter, Ruth, recalls that he only finally retired, at the age of forty-six, 'after seeing yet another friend [Bill Whitehouse] die, this time in a burning field [at Reims].' He turned, instead, to yacht racing:

> He would assume a whole new persona when racing yachts: aggressively determined to succeed, come what may! He was passionate in all he did; skiing, supporting Stoke City, collecting antiques, reading, beautiful women (he was married three times), country music, jogging and teaching his children to drive like racing drivers. He was always up for anything! He had a huge passion for life. When his garages failed at the time of the oil crisis, he simply turned around and started working equally hard at the second-hand car trade and he worked at this right up to his death.

Duncan Hamilton, who retired from racing around the same time as Nixon, became an outstanding sports car driver, notably in C and D-type Jaguars, winning Le Mans in 1953 with a broken nose, having hit a bird at 130 mph. His garage business selling classic cars was taken over by his son and still flourishes. The painting he donated of himself racing a Lago-Talbot at Silverstone in 1951 still adorns the walls of one of his favourite watering-holes, the Jersey Arms, Middleton Stoney. He died in 1994, aged seventy-four.

Opposite: Leslie Johnson's ERA GP2, the fastest car in first practice in the Race on the Runways, revisiting Silverstone in 2014.

Sam Gilbey, a fellow Maserati driver in 1948, raced no more at international meetings, but enjoyed several RAC Rallies before retiring to Spain. Back in England in poor health, he still regularly drove up from Ascot to Silverstone thanks to Jimmy Brown, who, coming across Gilbey struggling on foot towards the BRDC clubhouse, gave him immediate permission to park beside it for the rest of his days. Gilbey outlived Brown by several years, dying in 1995, aged eighty-seven.

* * *

The five surviving Grand Prix drivers – Bob Ansell, Toulo de Graffenried, Geoff Richardson, Tony Rolt and Roy Salvadori

– all returned in 1998, when Silverstone celebrated the fiftieth anniversary of the Race of the Runways with a wonderful parade of many of the original cars at the Coys Historic Festival. The amiable Bob Ansell, who retired from racing early, had moved with his family, on the sale of the Ansell Brewery, to a village in the Cotswolds, from where he long indulged his passion for shooting and country pursuits and often visited Silverstone. He died in 2004, aged eighty-six. Toulo de Graffenried had had the satisfaction of winning the Silverstone Grand Prix of 1949, driving the latest Maserati, and in 1950–56 competed in twenty-three World Championship races. He subsequently ran his

Left: The British bulldog spirit: Gordon and his wife, Marjorie. (*Marjorie Watson*)

Opposite: ERA GP1, the car that let Peter Walker down during first practice in 1948, revisiting Silverstone in 2014, where, in the hands of Duncan Ricketts, it came an impressive third in the ERA 80th Anniversary Trophy.

exclusive car dealership, selling Alfa Romeos, Rolls Royces and Ferraris. During the 1970s and 1980s he was a popular figure on the Formula 1 scene, working for Malboro as a corporate ambassador. He died in 2007 at ninety-two.

Geoff Richardson raced on with his home-built creations that he impishly called RRAs (Richardson Racing Automobiles). In 1951, his RRA crashed badly at Dundrod, hospitalising him for three months and severely exacerbating his wartime injuries, but he eventually recovered and was to remain competitive till his late thirties in non-championship Formula 1 and Formula Libre events. He later went air racing for twenty years and won the prestigious King's Cup. 'At times I wasn't too popular as I raced to win and applied motor racing principles,' he told writer Anthony Pritchard. 'If there was a bit of a hole between aircraft I'd go through it. In motor racing you could trust the other drivers but it wasn't the same in air racing. Some of the competitors were all over the place.' He was undeterred by the eventual amputation of one leg, reckoning the artificial replacement cured the limp he had always had since the wartime injury. He specially modified two artificial legs in his Worcestershire workshops, 'one for driving and one for country sports'. (He won the first BRDC clay pigeon shooting event.) He retired from his garage business in 1991, but continued working on engines. He went on flying, too, from his own airstrip near Shelsey Walsh, buying a new plane as late as 2000 and often landing it at Silverstone, where his tall, gangling figure was well-known in the BRDC Suite. Just before he died in 2007 at the age of eighty-two, he was wedding a 3-litre chassis to a 4.5-litre engine 'to create the Bentley of Bentleys'.

As the son of a Brigadier-General and a brewery heiress, Tony Rolt was well qualified to be a gentleman racer, but such were his talents that the Alfa Romeo 'bimotore' was the last car he himself had to buy. He enjoyed many successes in international sports car racing, especially at Le Mans with Duncan Hamilton, before retiring in 1955, shortly after witnessing the disaster there in which eighty people died. He had resigned his Army commission in 1948 to found a company specialising in advanced automotive technologies, later going into partnership with the tractor magnate Harry Ferguson in four-wheel drive projects, which included the Formula 1 car with which Stirling Moss won the Oulton Park Gold Cup. Rolt's company became a major technology partner with many leading manufacturers in the 1980s. In retirement he was able to pursue his hobbies of skiing and shooting and take pleasure in his son Stuart's chairmanship of the BRDC, a club of which Tony Rolt had been a member for over seventy years on his death in 2008 at the age of eighty-nine.

Roy Francesco Salvadori, the longest surviving competitor of the Race of the Runways, was to compete for a further seventeen seasons, becoming one of the greatest British Formula 1 drivers never to win a Grand Prix (out of forty-seven World Championship starts). He somehow managed to be in the wrong car at the wrong time. He was also a very fine sports car driver, winning Le Mans in an Aston Martin in 1959. He later managed Jochen Rindt and John Surtees in the Cooper Formula 1 Team of 1966/67, before concentrating on his garage businesses and retiring to Monaco, where he had a flat overlooking the Grand Prix course. A lifelong friend of Bernie Ecclestone, he died in Monaco in 2012, aged ninety.

CHAPTER 17

Gigi Villoresi was present again at Silverstone for the Grand Prix of 1949 and would have won it but for engine problems. Alberto Ascari was unavoidably absent, still recovering from injuries after crashing his Maserati in South America, though the car itself, after a hasty repair job, was present, driven by its new owner, Fred Ashmore. The two Italians were both back at Silverstone later that year for the first Daily Express International Trophy (which Alberto won), but no longer in Maseratis, for Gigi had just done a surprise deal, on their joint behalf, to drive for Enzo Ferrari. It was a move that would bring Alberto World Championship titles in 1952 and 1953 (including victories both years at Silverstone) and see him overtake his friend and mentor as the leading Italian driver.

Gigi himself won eighteen more Grands Prix after the Race on the Runways, as well as the Mille Miglia, but it was a time marred by several bad crashes. In July 1950, at the *Grand Prix de Nations* held on public roads in Geneva, Gigi's misfiring Ferrari spun on oil, hit some straw bales, climbed 20 feet into the air and somersaulted, throwing Gigi into the middle of the road. It ended up among the densely packed crowd, killing three spectators and injuring another thirty. Gigi was in a coma for three days but slowly recovered, though he lost the end of the index finger on his right hand and would not race again for eight months. Alberto was at his bedside as Gigi regained consciousness. 'Now don't you see that I was right!' he exclaimed. Shortly before the race, Alberto, whose many superstitions included fear of black cats, had begged Gigi in vain not to pick up a black kitten.

The two friends left Ferrari for Lancia in 1954, but in testing a Lancia Aurelia on the public roads Gigi had another bad accident, ending up pinned underneath the car in the Italian countryside until a helpful farmer produced a couple of oxen to move it. Amazingly, though again badly injured, Gigi won an international sports car race only two months later, beating both Alberto and the rising young Italian star, Castellotti, in similar Lancias.

The Lancia D50 Grand Prix car was just beginning to be competitive, giving Alberto wins at Turin and Naples, when, in May 1955, he had a shocking accident, losing control at the Harbour Chicane while leading at Monaco, and plunging through the bales into the sea. An oil slick and a circle of bubbles marked the spot where Alberto and his Lancia had disappeared, and then, miraculously, up came the well-known blue helmet and the badly shaken Alberto was rescued.

Suffering from bruises and a broken nose, Alberto was a surprise visitor to Monza four days later, where Castellotti was testing a Ferrari sports car they were to share the coming weekend. On the spur of the moment, Alberto decided to try it himself, and though he had not brought his lucky blue helmet and racing shirt with him, he borrowed Castellotti's helmet and casually set off in jacket and tie. Gigi, watching from the stands, was shocked that the superstitious Alberto was setting off without his own 'lucky' equipment but was too far away to intervene. Twice the silver Ferrari passed by the stands and all seemed well. Then silence. News quickly arrived that the Ferrari had gone off the road on the inside of the Vialone curve (where there were no barriers to protect a car from the trees). They found Alberto unconscious, lying on his back on a grass verge, some distance from the badly damaged car. Two separate parts of Castellotti's helmet lay by themselves on the road. Alberto, still with a faint pulse, was gently lifted onto a stretcher and into an ambulance, which, with Gigi beside him, headed swiftly for the nearest hospital. But before they reached it, Alberto gave a small shudder and died in Gigi's arms.

Alberto had told Gigi several times recently that he would not live through the year; that his father had died at thirty-six and so would he. Each time Gigi had laughed and told him not to be stupid. But there he was now, distraught and disbelieving, mechanically picking up the hospital phone and asking his sister Rosa to go round to Mietta and break the terrible news of her husband's death.

Milan mourned a second time for an Ascari. The square facing the church of San Carlo al Corso was packed with silently grieving fans as the cortège arrived from Monza and the coffin was carried into the church by Gigi and other Ambrosiana drivers. The next day, a million mourners witnessed the funeral procession pass through the city's streets, with the famous blue helmet on top of the coffin, on the way to the Monumental Cemetery. Fifteen carriages were needed to carry all the flowers and wreaths. Gigi supported Mietta, as her husband was buried beside his illustrious father. A bronze bust of the son in due course joined that of the father.

Alberto's gentle and attractive personality had led to his idolisation almost as much as his many achievements. Unaltered by fame and allowing himself no airs or graces, he had become one of the Italian people's greatest sporting favourites, a double World Champion who could have been taken for a pastry cook, aptly and most affectionately nicknamed *Il Ciccio* ('The Chubby One').

Gigi was devastated by his death. When, four months later, Monza hosted the Italian Grand Prix, he turned out for Lancia for the days of practice but opted not to race (with 'tyre problems'). The next year Gigi left Lancia and returned to Maserati, driving 250Fs of an uncompetitive nature. Though he came to Silverstone in 1956, his sixth-place Maserati was five laps down on Fangio's winning Lancia-Ferrari. That year he managed just four laps at Monza before handing his Maserati over to Jo Bonnier. And then, at the *Gran Premio di Roma*, held among the sand dunes and pine forests of the Castelfusano circuit outside Ostia, he crashed his Maserati sports car with such serious consequences that even he was unable to race again. He managed a remarkable victory in the Acropolis Rally in 1958 and then, at forty-nine, he finally retired after a career that had begun in 1931.

For a while he flourished in Milan in his new life with an Innocenti-Mini dealership, giving Alberto's son, Tonino Ascari, a job for a time as he embarked on a short racing career of his own. But Gigi was always too trusting and generous, always careless with money and an easy prey to the less scrupulous. Badly cheated by a business partner, he lost all he had. A period of utter misery followed until finally an old friend, Maria Teresa de Filippis, learning that he was in dire need and unable to pay his rent, swiftly contacted a priest in Modena, Don Sergio Mantovani, a wonderful character, passionately devoted to motor racing. Mantovani had just founded 'the House of Joy and Sunshine', a rest home in Modena, and there, in 1994, at the age of eighty-five, Gigi at last found a sanctuary that gave him back his dignity. When he died at Modena three years later, over 1,000 people attended his funeral at Don Sergio's church of Santa Caterina. He was buried in the cemetery of Albareto on the city's outskirts.

In old age he was frequently asked about Alberto, but would say little. It was still too painful. He told one biographer he had little to add to what he had written to Alberto forty years earlier, at the time of his death:

Despite all that happened on that sad afternoon of May 26 I am incapable of saying goodbye to you. It seems you are still there, beside me. We spent so much of our lives together in the warm embrace of friendship that everything seems to have stopped without you. Do you remember the tests, the trials, the Grand Prix, the journeys, the chattering, the hours of rest? And the endless mutual decisions, because we felt that we shared the same journey in life?

Gigi and Alberto's 'same journey' in 1948: approaching Chapel, leaving Segrave and rounding Copse. (*Ferret Fotographics and BRDC*)